Too Risky!

Too Risky!

Jim Davidson's
secret joke book

 Robson Books

Cartoons by ·MADDOCKS·

Designed by Anna Lovell

First published in Great Britain in 1986 by Robson Books Ltd.,
Bolsover House, 5-6 Clipstone Street, London W1P 7EB.

Copyright © 1986 Jim Davidson

British Library Cataloguing in Publication Data

Davidson, Jim
  Too Risky!
  I. Title
  828.'91407 PR6054.A86/

  ISBN 0-86051-399-8

Typeset by Bookworm Typesetting, Manchester
Printed in Great Britain by
St Edmundsbury Press Ltd, Bury St Edmunds, Suffolk
Bound by Dorstel Press Ltd, Harlow, Essex

Contents

Introduction

It was a bloke at school who gave me the idea for one of the characters I made up to use in my act, a stupid cockney called Alex. He used to talk quite seriously about doing the craziest things. I remember him telling us one day he was going to do over a bank, 'the Barclays, the Westminster, or the Midland . . . but not the Lloyds – too risky.'

He was a right nutcase. Why Lloyds was different I never found out, but his line 'too risky' stuck with me right from entertaining mates in the school playground, through doing stand-up routines in the pubs and clubs of south-east London (I used to have a regular spot at the old Black Bull in Lewisham for six quid a turn), to opening my act recently in America by telling the audience, 'The F-111s bombing Libya have done us a great favour – it's kept you pain-in-the-arse Americans out of London!' That had them gasping a little bit, but it went all right. If it hadn't, it would have been tough and I'd have had an early night. In my business you never apologise for a joke.

I've always enjoyed blue humour and other risky jokes, and my act is all about making people laugh by taking chances and cracking jokes about those embarrassing things they don't like talking about. Like what do you do when you go to the toilet and there's no lock on the door? You have to sit there with a long left leg, until you try it in a pub where the door opens out . . .

During the pit strike I used to ask if there were any miners in the house and if there were I'd tell them, 'Then get back to work, you lazy buggers', which had them busting their sides. Of course there was always one misery who wouldn't see the funny side and got the hump when I had a go at Arthur Scargill, but, I ask you, how can you trust a man who tries to cover up his bald patch?

Still, I try to be careful about what I say when there are kids in the audience, which is why my pantomimes never have any of the jokes that go into my live adult performances. It's the same with television. There you go into people's homes which isn't the same as having them

come to see you, so I'm always having to hold back the really good jokes to avoid anything that 'normal' people would think offensive.

There are some people (women mostly) who get stroppy at some of the jokes I like and put into my live shows. Not long ago a woman wrote and told me she'd walked out after ten minutes and she picked on one joke that had really offended her, or so she claimed – the only trouble was that that gag had come right at the end of the show!

Pain-in-the-neck do-gooders – they're the ones who also get up-tight. People impersonate me and tell jokes about me but I never let that rub me up the wrong way. It's like my character Chalkie, the dim-witted black guy who's always falling off his bike and who has twice as many gold teeth as anyone else. Some people might say jokes about him are racist. All I can say is that black people laugh at him more than white, and I've found that jokes about Chalkie get any audience going. People are always asking for them, whether they're as innocent as the first one I ever told:

> 'Where do you work, Chalkie?' I asked him.
> 'I work for Cheesus.'
> 'The Lord Jesus?'
> 'No, Kraft Cheesus.'

Or a lot nearer the nerve, like this one:

> Chalkie had terrible trouble with his dick.
> It kept itching. He kept scratching and one day the bit that stops your hand shooting off the end fell off. So he went to see the doctor.
> 'What's the matter,' asked the doc.
> 'It's my dick, it's fallen off.'
> 'Have you got it with you?'
> 'Yeah – it's in my pocket.' And he got it out and gave it to him.
> The doctor took a sniff and said, 'Gor, dear. This is a mistake. You've given me a marshmallow.'

> 'Don't be silly,' said Chalkie, 'I ate that coming
> up the stairs.'

Chalkie's always been good for a laugh and in my experience it's very seldom that anyone black complains about him.

Nowadays my act is made up of my favourite jokes, the ones I've found have worked best with all sorts of audiences. Humour is universal and I reckon if you find the right combination of material you can give the same performance to anyone who speaks English and they'll laugh along with you. I might have to speak slower to an audience in America and Australia, so that they can get used to my accent, but apart from that the act stays the same.

There are audiences which have certain 'in' jokes that have a special significance for them and I like to include those too. On my trips down to the Falklands I played gymnasiums in Port Stanley, huts out in the camps and remote outposts on the tops of mountains – where a helicopter dropped me off if I was lucky and there wasn't too much cloud; otherwise I had a four-hour ride in a tracked vehicle up the mountainside – in front of squaddies to whom a joke like this had a special meaning:

> A policeman dies and goes to heaven where St
>   Peter asks him, 'What do you do?'
> 'I'm a policeman. I was in the Flying Squad.'
> 'That's great. God'll be ever so pleased, he
>   really likes policemen. Go and sit beside him
>   and talk to him.'
> Twenty minutes later another bloke arrives at
>   the Pearly Gates and says, 'I'm a policeman, I
>   got hit by a runaway car coming up Vine
>   Street in the West End.'
> 'Great! God will be pleased. Go and sit next to
>   him and have a chat.'
> Half an hour goes by and there's another
>   knock. St Peter looks out and the bloke says,
>   'I'm a policeman and I've died.'

'What sort of policeman are you?'
'I'm a Ministry of Defence policeman.'
'Oh, great. Look after these gates while I go out
    for a piss.'

That was told to me by a military policeman and I don't
suppose I'd have heard it if I hadn't been working with the
army then. (I had the idea of doing a show based on six
weeks' training with the Marines and giving a concert on
the last night based on all the material I'd gathered – but I
don't think I'd have lived through it all to have made it on
stage at the end.)
   It's always been a cliché that there's no such thing as an
original joke. Yes, there are thousands of good old ones and
I know some of the best, but I'm often coming across new
gags, like this one I heard only the other day:

A pornographic film starlet is in hospital having
    a baby.
'It's got a black head,' the doctor tells her.
'Well, I did star in some porno films with
    blacks. Maybe some of it's worn off?'
'Yes, but it's got light brown arms.'
'Yeah – there were a few Pakistanis in those
    films too.'
'And a yellow body?'
'Some Chinks as well – I had them too.'
'Apart from that it's quite a healthy baby. It's
    crying naturally anyway.'
'Thank God for that – I thought you were going
    to say it's barking.'

That's been added to all the others I've picked up over the
years, one more for the collection which is now a sort of
huge menu – a massive Chinese menu, if you like, that has
hundreds of different bits to try and enjoy but which still
leaves you feeling hungry for more. That's why the jokes in
this book have been arranged like a Chinese menu with
Won Ton Soup filled with quick-fire startlers to get you in
the mood, followed by *Sweet and Sour* gags about kids,

Spare Ribs (wisecracks on women), *Prawn Balls* which hang (sorry!) on us blokes, and so on through the list.

So, to whet your appetite here are a couple of Chinese crackers to set you up before you get into the menu:

A man in a Chinese restaurant one night called over one of the waiters and said, 'This chicken's rubbery!'
'Ah,' said the waiter, 'thank you velly much.'

Another Chinese waiter served a customer a plate of soup with his thumb sticking in it.
'Oy,' said the customer, 'your thumb's in my soup.'

'I got leumatism in this thumb and the doctor
     says to keep it warm.'
'Well, stick it up your arse, mate.'
'I do when I'm in kitchen.'

There, not too lisky! Now see how you get on with the lest
of the goodies.

What's a clunt?
     *Someone who tries to leave a Chinese restaurant without
     paying.*

WON TON SOUP

or Startlers

Won Ton Soup

Here's a collection of quick-fire one-liners to get you going. Jokes like this started life in the days of music hall comics, when the 'I say, I say, I say' double-acts were popular. They were perfected by northern comics and today Bernard Manning is my favourite master of the one-line gag. Down in London the current trend of developing and elongating what started as a one-line joke developed from a comedian called Peter Demmer. He was at his height here in the late 60's and early 70's. I used to go down to a pub called the Adam and Eve to watch him and he'd take a one-liner and make it into ten minutes, inventing all the characters and acting them. In my own act I use one-liners in a machine-gun, attacking style, one after the other, plastering the audience with a burst of short gags to vary the pace of the act. In that way you get them laughing right from the first thing you say and work off some of your own nerves at the same time.

Customer: 'Chinese waiter! There's a dead fly in my won ton soup.' **Chinese waiter:** 'What do you expect for twenty-five pence? Dead eagle?'

What's the definition of lockjaw?
> *Never having to say you're sorry.*

What do you call a man with two dicks?
> *Lucky.*

What do you call a man with eleven dicks?
> *Bobby Robson.*

Why was the man with five dicks pleased?
> *Because his underpants fitted him like a glove.*

What's the world's yuckiest film?
Chain-saw Vasectomy.

What happened to the woman whose husband didn't know
the difference between a Pyrex and a Durex?
She had a baby with a glass head.

How can you tell Dolly Parton's children?
They're the ones with stretch marks round their mouths.

What's the best way to stop flies spreading disease?
Keep 'em zipped up!

Why did the necrophiliac have to give it up?
Some rotten sod split on him.

Why is artificial insemination so successful?
Because there's no chance of a cock-up.

Why do Irishmen wear two Durex?
To be sure, to be sure.

What do you call a prostitute's kid?
A brothel sprout.

What do you give a constipated canary?
Chirrup of figs.

What's another name for wife-swapping?
Four-play.

Why was the girl called Angel Delight?
Because she was so easy to make.

WHAT DO YOU CALL A GAY MONKEY?

A chimp-pansy.

What do you give the girl who has everything?
A very wide berth.

What happened to the French lorry driver who swerved to avoid a child?
He fell off the bed.

'Do you ever talk to your wife when you're making love?'
Only if she telephones.'

What's the definition of a eunuch?
A man cut out to be a bachelor.

What do you call a well-hung Irish male stripper?
Miles O'Toole.

What happened when the vegetarian nudist stood too close to the fire?
He had a nut roast.

What's the best way to get into a sleeping bag?
Wake her up.

What did Long John Silver enjoy doing best?
Trying to get his log over.

What's the definition of a mistress?
Something in between a mister and a mattress.

What does an elephant keep in its trunk?
About a yard and a half of snot.

Why did Humpty Dumpty have a great fall?
To make up for his lousy summer.

What is the definition of macho?
Jogging home from your vasectomy.

What do you call a queer Australian?
One who prefers women to beer.

What's the true meaning of the phrase 'vice versa'?
>   *Dirty poetry.*

What do you call a jockstrap made of Axminster?
>   *Ball-to-ball carpeting.*

What do you get if you cross Quasimodo with Dolly Parton?
>   *The Hunchfront of Notre Dame.*

What does Quasimodo enjoy doing most?
>   *Humping.*
Why did he give it up?
>   *Because of his bad back.*

Why did the queer Australian leave his wife?
>   *Because he wanted to go back to Sydney.*

What sticks out of a man's pyjamas, has hair round it and is long enough to stick a hat on?
>   *His head!*

What does a man do standing up, a woman sitting down and a dog on three legs?
>   *Shake hands.*

What do you call a cannibal who eats his mother's sister?
>   *An aunt-eater.*

Why do farts smell?
>   *For the benefit of the deaf.*

How did the Irishman burn his face?
>   *Bobbing for chips.*

How would you describe good, clean fun?
>   *No good at all.*

Why do firemen have bigger balls than policemen?
>   *Because they sell more tickets.*

Why does Neil Kinnock prefer meeting the Pope to meeting Arthur Scargill?
> *He only has to kiss his HAND.*

If you're squeezing a cricket ball in your left hand and a cricket ball in your right hand, what have you got in front of you?
> *A cricket with tears in its eyes.*

What's the difference between a sewing-machine and Dolly Parton running for a bus?
> *A sewing-machine only has one bobbin'.*

What is the definition of circumcision?
> *What cuts off the Jews from the Gentiles.*

What do you call an Irish-Jewish gnome?
> *A lepracohen.*

Why did the little boy ask the chemist for a box of Tampax?
> *Because his sister said that with Tampax you could swim, and ride a bike . . .*

What is a lesbian?
> *A mannish depressive with delusions of gender.*

What do you call an uncircumcised Jewish baby?
> *A girl.*

What did Whistler say when he found his mother on the floor?
> *'You must be off your rocker!'*

What's the definition of a perfect lover?
> *A Frenchman with a nine-inch tongue who can breathe through his ears.*

Why did the young boy insist on inserting his willy into a box of biscuits?
> *He was f-ing crackers.*

What's the difference between a cross-eyed cowboy and a constipated owl?
>*A cross-eyed cowboy shoots but can't hit . . .*

What can six men do that three women can't?
>*Pee in a bucket at the same time.*

What's the difference between a barrow-boy and a dachshund?
>*The barrow-boy bawls his wares out on the pavement . . .*

What did the policeman say when he caught his wife in bed with three men?
>*Hello, 'ello, 'ello.'*

What do you get if you cross a parrot with a seagull?
>*A bird that craps on holidaymakers, then says sorry.*

Why do spiders taste like chewing gum?
>*Because they're Wrigglies.*

What's the difference between a Scottish lodger and VD?
>*You can get rid of VD.*

What can an ostrich, a pelican and a flamingo do that the gas and electricity boards can do too?
>*Shove their bills up their arses.*

What's the difference between the M1 and Terry Wogan?
>*You can turn off the M1.*

Why don't Scotsmen play dominoes in a pub.
>*They're scared of knocking in case the landlord comes over.*

My wife has had so many face-lifts that the next time they'll have to lower her body.

Why was the Irishman
jumping up and down on a
hedgehog?

*He was trying to get
a conker out of it.*

'Mary, I think your husband dresses nattily.'
  '*Nathalie who?*'

What's the difference between having a light on and having
a hard on?
  You can have a light on all night.

What did the sweet-toothed vampire like for 'afters'?
  Diabetics.

What do you call a dog with no legs?
  Anything you like – it still won't come to you.

What's got seven eyes but can't see?
  Three blind mice and half a sheep's head.

My wife goes for a tramp in the woods every evening.
So far, he's always managed to get away.

Why did the man who had a dog with no legs call it 'Woodbine'?
Because he used to take it out for a drag.

How can you tell which clan a Scotsman belongs to?
Lift up his kilt – if he's got two quarter-pounders, he's a McDonalds.

Why did the gay Scotsman go to Indian?
He was waiting for a mon soon.

What was Ghenghis Khan's impotent younger brother called?
Ghenghis Khan't.

Why did the eunuch give up playing cricket?
He kept getting no-balled.

Did you know that the marriage of two lighthouse keepers was on the rocks?

Why was the rabbi sacked from the garage?
He kept cutting two inches off the exhaust pipes.

What's the height of cheek?
Peeing through a person's letterbox, then knocking on the door to ask how far it went.

What does a gynaecologist say when he's first introduced?
Dilated to make your acquaintance.

Why did the gynaecologist get into trouble with his wife?
Because he kept working late at the orifice.

A man who swallowed a dud coin yesterday is to be charged today with passing counterfeit money.

What do you get if you cross a birthday cake with a tin of baked beans?
A cake that blows all the candles out by itself.

> **Have you heard that eggs are going up?**
> **The hens have lost all sense of direction.**

What did the giraffe say when it strolled into the cocktail bar?
> *'The highballs are on me!'*

What was Snow White's favourite drink?
> *Seven-up.*

What do a soya bean and a vibrator have in common?
> *They're both meat substitutes.*

Why do prostitutes never vote?
> *They couldn't care less WHO gets in.*

What did the Irishman do when his wife put mirrors on the bedroom ceiling?
> *He shaved on his back.*

What do you get if you cross a Jew with a Scotsman?
> *Rabbi Burns.*

Why are rectal thermometers banned in America?
> *Because they cause brain damage.*

Why did the Irishman dip his dick into a liqueur before sex?
> *To practise Cointreauception.*

> *Chalkie had diarrhoea once and thought he was melting.*

SWEET AND SOUR

or
Children's Chortles

Sweet and Sour

There's a lot of truth in the old saying 'Children will get you hung', especially when it comes to kids' jokes. They seem to combine childish innocence with the sort of frankness that can often be very embarrassing for their parents. One of the stock characters is the cheeky little kid in school, the little lad who's asked by the teacher, 'What happened when Moses went to Mount Olive?' and answers, 'Popeye smacked him in the mouth.' Kids can come out with some funny things in real life. The little son of a friend of mine got hiccoughs and told his father in alarm, 'Dad, I keep stopping.' They can also show they know more about the world than their parents ever imagine. A little boy told his father, 'Dad, there's a daddy longlegs on top of a mummy longlegs.' 'Don't be stupid,' said his father, 'there's no such thing as a mummy longlegs.' So the kid trod on the insect in disgust saying 'Ugh, poof, eh?' If you're playing to an audience of adults, most of whom will be parents, jokes about kids always go down well.

Six-year-old twins Dicky and Fanny were splashing happily together in their bath when Dicky said, 'I'm going to give you a good ducking!'

'Huh!' came Fanny's reply. 'You can't even *say* the word properly!'

★　★　★

A policeman caught a rather nasty little boy with a penknife in one hand and a squirrel in the other. 'Now listen here,' he said, 'whatever you do to that poor, defenceless creature I shall personally do to *you*.'

'In that case,' replied the boy, 'I'll just kiss its arse and let it go!'

★　★　★

'Dad! Dad!' shouted the little boy running excitedly into the living room. 'I've got my eye on a bike for my birthday!'

Without looking up from his newspaper, his father replied, 'Well, son, keep your eye on it. You'll never get your *arse* on it.'

* * *

Little Jimmy saw his father walking round the bathroom without any clothes for the first time. Filled with wonder, he pointed at his father's courting tackle and asked, 'What's that thing, Dad?'

'Why, that's a spaceship, son,' replied his father with a smile.

'It's not a very big spaceship, is it, Dad?' said the boy.

'Not yet,' replied his dad. 'But it sure gets bigger nearer Ma's!' [Mars]

* * *

The little lad was bragging about his big brother's musical capabilities. 'Our Jonathan can play the piano by ear,' he said smugly.

'That's nothing,' said his friend. 'Our Trevor can fiddle with his willy!'

* * *

A teacher was asking her infants' class whether any of them had a father who could do unusual things.

'Yes, miss,' said one tiny tot. 'My dad can blow smoke rings through his bum.'

Embarrassed, the young teacher stammered that that was impossible.

'No it's not,' said the youngster. 'I've seen the nicotine on his underpants.'

* * *

Accompanying her mother to the hairdresser's, a little girl was unwrapping a toffee when she accidentally dropped it on the floor. As she bent down to pick it up and pop it into her mouth, the man who was styling her mother's hair shrieked in horror, 'Do you know you've got hair all over your sweetie?'

'Yeth,' said the little girl. 'And I'm only nine!'

★ ★ ★

A young girl was being bothered by unwanted attention in the cinema, so she called out, 'Take your hand off my knee! No, not you, *you*!'

NO, NOT YOU, <u>YOU</u>

'Mummy, where did I come from?' asked little Jimmy one day.

Thinking quickly, his doting mother replied, 'You came from a sugar bowl, my sweet one.'

Later that day, Jimmy approached his father. 'Daddy,' he said, 'Mummy says I came from a sugar bowl ...'

'That's about the size of it, son,' replied the cynical father.

★   ★   ★

'Mummy, is our new *au pair* bionic?' asked little Jenny sweetly.

'Heavens, no!' replied her mother. 'Whatever made you ask that?'

'Well,' said the little girl, 'last night I heard Daddy telling Uncle Norman that he'd just screwed the behind off the *au pair*!'

★   ★   ★

Little Jimmy was pestering his mother to take him to the loo but, being very busy, she snapped, 'Ask grandad to take you!' 'I'd rather go with granny,' said Jimmy, 'her hand shakes more!'

★   ★   ★

A young schoolmaster rushed into the headmaster's study in a distraught state. 'Oh, sir!' he cried. 'I've just caught three small boys trying to see how high they could pee up the side of the classroom wall!'

'And what did you do?' asked the headmaster calmly.

'What did I do? I hit the ceiling!' said the teacher.

'Oh, *good shot*!' said the headmaster. 'That's one up for the staff!'

★   ★   ★

Ten-year-old Willy shocked a pretty young schoolteacher on her first day by asking her if she minded if he smoked a cigarette in class.

'Certainly I mind! Do you want to get me into trouble?' she replied.

'I'm game if you are,' said little Willy eagerly.

★　★　★

A mother noticed that her children and their friends had disappeared from the living room, so she called out to find out where they were.
　'We're in the cellar!' came the reply.
　'What are you doing down there?' she asked.
　'Making love,' they answered.
　'That's nice, dears. Don't fight.'

★　★　★

A city girl saw a cow for the first time . . . and thought it was a bull that had swallowed a glove.

★　★　★

There was a young man from Cape Horn
　Who wished that he'd never been born.
　And he wouldn't have been, if his father had seen
　That the end of his rubber was torn.

Here's to the girl who lives on the the hill . . . She won't – but her sister will!

Jack and Jill went up the hill
　To fetch a pail of water.
　Jill came down with half a crown
　But it wasn't for fetching water.

★　★　★

A rabbi stumbled over a small boy who was playing on the steps of the local synagogue. 'Get out of my way you young whipper-snapper!' he roared.
　'Sod off, you big whopper-snipper!' retorted the boy.

★　★　★

36

Two little girls were paddling at the seaside.

'Oh!' said one. 'Aren't your feet dirty!'

'Yes,' replied her friend. 'We didn't come last year.'

★ ★ ★

A schoolgirl with uncontrollable hiccups went to the doctor to see if he could do something to stop them. The canny doctor examined her all over and then pronounced gravely, 'I've got news for you, miss. You're pregnant.'

The girl fainted on the spot and when she came round a few minutes later she wailed, 'Oh, doctor – am I *really* pregnant?'

'No,' replied the doctor. 'But it cured your hiccups, didn't it!'

★ ★ ★

It was the young cannibal's first taste of a missionary.

'Well,' said his proud father. 'Are you enjoying it?'

'Mm-mm,' said the boy. 'I'm having a ball.'

★ ★ ★

Two sixteen-year-olds walked into a pub after their first love-making session in the park.

'What will you have to drink?' asked the boy.

'A half of lager and lime, please,' said the girl.

The landlord suspected that the girl was under-age, and said sternly, '*You've* had it!'

'Yes,' she replied coyly. 'And doesn't it make you thirsty!'

★ ★ ★

Two little boys were talking in Hollywood.

'What's your new mother like?' asked one.

'OK, I suppose,' said his friend. 'Do you know her?'

'Oh, yes,' said the first boy. 'We had her last year.'

★ ★ ★

Little Jenny was playing in the garden while her father cut the grass.

'Dad,' she called, 'what are those two insects doing?'

37

'Well,' he replied, 'remember what I told you about the birds and bees? That's what they're doing.'

'But those aren't birds and bees,' said Jenny.

'No, they're daddy-longlegs.'

'Which one is the daddy-longlegs and which one is the mummy-longlegs?'

'They're both daddy-longlegs.'

Immediately Jenny stamped on the insects, and turned to her father: 'I'm not having *that* sort of thing in our garden!'

⋆　⋆　⋆

Did you hear about the little boy who took his nose apart?
He wanted to see what made it run.

⋆　⋆　⋆

What did the Scotsman do when he was asked to donate to an orphanage?
Sent two orphans.

⋆　⋆　⋆

My family was very, very poor when I was a child. So poor, in fact, that my brother was made in Hong Kong.

⋆　⋆　⋆

What is the opposite of minimum?
Minidad.

⋆　⋆　⋆

My sister's just given up her boyfriend.
She had to – he was tall, dark and hands . . .

⋆　⋆　⋆

A boy, cuddling a girl, asked her if he was the first boy she had ever kissed. The girl pushed him away, looked at him closely, and replied, 'You might be, your face looks familiar.'

⋆　⋆　⋆

A little boy went back to school after three days' absence. His teacher asked him why he had been away, and the little

38

boy said, 'My dad was burnt.'

'Oh, said the teacher, 'not seriously, I hope.'

'Well,' he said, 'they don't mess about down at the crematorium, you know!'

★   ★   ★

A little boy was playing in the school yard at lunchtime with a little girl. 'Guess what I found behind the radiator in our classroom? A contraceptive!'

'What's a radiator?' asked the little girl.

★   ★   ★

Two lads were playing in the street where they lived when they saw a friend looking through the kitchen window of a near-by house. He called them over, 'Quick! There's a man and woman in there fighting!'

The two boys ran to the window and looked in. They're not fighting,' said one. 'They're making love.'

'And not very well,' said the other.

★   ★   ★

Today it's young girls who sow their wild oats all night. And in the morning they pray for crop failure.

39

★ ★ ★

Jimmy's parent's explained the facts of life to him, but were too embarrassed to do the same for his five-year-old brother.

'Jimmy,' begged his father, 'you'll tell him all that we've just told you about the birds and the bees, won't you?'

Jimmy agreed, and that evening before he and his brother went to sleep, he said, 'You know what Dad and Mum do every night in bed, don't you?'

'Yes, of course I do,' said his little brother.

'Well, so do the birds and bees,' said Jimmy.

★ ★ ★

A young Roman Catholic boy was talking to.his priest, and asked him whether it was truly a sin to sleep with a girl.

'No,' replied the priest. 'The trouble is that you young men don't sleep.'

When asked why the Children of Israel made a Golden Calf, one little boy told his teacher he thought it must be because there wasn't enough gold to make a cow.

★ ★ ★

What's the best way to tell the sex of a hormone?
Take its genes off.

★ ★ ★

Chalkie met another of his mates when they were out pushing their children along in prams. Chalkie had a nice little black baby but his mate's one was light brown and he asked Chalkie, 'How come you've got a black baby, Chalkie, and I've got a light brown one?' 'Well, Leroy,' said Chalkie, 'have you got a white woman?' 'No, I've got a black woman from the West Indies.' 'Oh . . . are you well endowed, then,' Chalkie asked.' 'No,' said Leroy, 'I've only got a little one.' 'Well, that's your trouble. You're letting in too much light round the sides.'

40

SPARE RIBS

or Wisecracks on Women

Spare Ribs

I think there's something in the English character that doesn't like to see women making fools of themselves. That's probably why there aren't as many women comedians here as there are in America, where there are a number of very successful comediennes. That doesn't mean that the English don't like laughing at jokes about women, but they seem to prefer them to be told by men. Even happily married men love jokes about miserable wives, and mother-in-law jokes are in a class all of their own. I've found that women in my audiences will laugh at dirty jokes every bit as enthusiastically as the men they're with, it's just that often they try to seem above all the filth.

One of the jokes that always gets a roar is set in the situation where the best jokes originate (especially the ones about women) – the pub. One bloke, talking to a mate of his as the lads were drinking at the bar, said, 'Look Charlie, I know we've been friends a long time, so I want to tell you, your wife's sitting over there with my missus and the girls. She's got a short skirt on and I can see that her knickers are full of holes.' 'I'll go over and tell her,' said Charlie, and gave her a right ticking off. 'What's the idea of coming in here showing me up with all holes in your knickers?' 'Well, it's not my fault. You don't give me any money to buy any knickers.' 'Right, here's twenty quid,' Charlie said. 'Now go and buy yourself loads of them.' After he'd gone back to the lads, the girls started talking about it and said, 'That ain't bad is it? Twenty quid just for having holes in your knickers.' 'No, it isn't,' said another of them, 'and my Bert's over there. I'll get some money out of him and I'll take mine off.' So she took them off and gave him a flash, and he ran over and said, 'Oy! What's the idea of coming in here and showing me up in front of all my mates?' 'Well, it's not my fault you don't give me any money to buy any knickers,' she said. 'Well, here's two quid,' said Bert, 'go out and get a comb and tidy yourself up.' That gets the biggest laugh from both the men and the women in the audience.

Driving into the car-park of a large motel, the commercial traveller was amazed at the over-abundance of Rolls Royces, Jaguars, Daimlers and a host of other expensive cars. What was strange was that there didn't seem to be anyone about to drive them. In fact, when he got inside the motel, he appeared to be the only customer.

He rang the bell at reception and the woman who owned the motel – a stunning blonde with an hour-glass figure and forty-inch bust – came to attend to him. As he was signing the register, he said, 'I hope you won't think I'm being nosy, but who owns all those large cars outside?'

'As a matter of fact they belong to me,' said the blonde.

'You must be extremely rich,' remarked the salesman.

'Not at all – I won them off men who have stayed here,' explained the woman. 'You see, I bet them that they can't do what my eight-year-old nephew Charles can do.'

'But that's silly!' remonstrated the man. 'Any grown man can do what a kid can do!'

'I'll bet my motel against your car that you can't,' replied the woman.

'OK – it's a bet!' said the salesman.

The woman called for her nephew. 'Right, Charles,' she said, 'kiss these.' And to the man's amazement, she took out her massive breasts, which the little lad started to kiss. 'Now it's *your* turn,' said the blonde to the salesman – who didn't need a second bidding!

'There! You see, I can do anything an eight-year-old can do!' he proclaimed, eagerly burrowing his head again between the woman's breasts.

'Not so fast,' said the woman. 'Charles, kiss this.' And she dropped her silk panties before the astonished salesman.

Charles did as requested. 'Not it's your turn again,' she said to the salesman, who went about his task all eagerness again, kissing the blonde's nether regions.

'There! I win!' he exclaimed delightedly. 'I *told* you any man can do anything a little boy can do! Have you got the deeds to the motel handy?'

'Not so fast!' said the blonde. 'There's one more thing. Charles – bend your willy in half and ask the gentleman for

Charles – bend your willy in half and ask the gentleman for his car keys.'

★ ★ ★

A lady was quarrelling with her maid, and the maid decided to tell her a few home truths.

'I'll tell you, madam,' she said, 'that your husband has told me himself that he thinks I'm a better housekeeper, cook and laundress than you are! *And* he thinks I'm prettier. But that's not all – I'm better than you are in bed!'

'I suppose my husband told you that too?' demanded the lady.

'No, he didn't,' replied the maid. 'The gardener told me.'

★ ★ ★

'Excuse me, madam, could you spare me a few moments for some research I'm doing? Could you tell me what you think of sex on television?'

'Very uncomfortable.'

★ ★ ★

Two neighbours were praising their new milkman. 'He's very good-looking, punctual and dresses so smartly,' said one.

'Yes, and so quickly, too!' replied the other.

★ ★ ★

A bald-headed man went to a prostitute with an expensive wig covering his hairless plate. They both stripped off and she turned off the lights. Just as they were about to make love, the man's wig slipped off in the dark and frantically he crawled about the bed searching for it. As his bald head brushed against the prostitute's she gasped and exclaimed: 'Aren't you a big boy! But wet it and I'll try it!'

★ ★ ★

Young Gladys was going for the first time to a holiday camp with some friends and her father was giving her some advice on how to protect herself from any amorous young wolves she might meet on holiday.

'Don't worry, Dad,' said Gladys, tapping the side of her head. 'I've got it up here.'

'I don't care *where* you've hidden it,' said her dad. 'Those buggers will still ruddy well find it!'

★ ★ ★

My mother-in-law is a very spiteful woman. When she caught rabies, she wrote down a list of the people she wanted to bite.

★ ★ ★

An old woman had failing eyesight and was peering through her spectacles, trying to discern the message contained in a telegram sent by her grandson.

'I say, is that an "I" or an "O" in that word there?' she said, nudging her husband.

The old man squinted at the telegram for several moments before pronouncing, 'It's an "O".'

'Bloody hell!' shouted the woman. 'Our Albert's *shot* himself!'

★ ★ ★

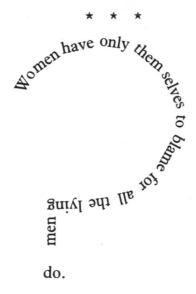

Women have only themselves to blame for all the lying men do.

They always ask questions.

A man walked into a pub one evening in a furious temper and said to a friend, 'That wife of mine is a liar!'

'What makes you think that?' asked the friend.

'She just told me she spent last night with Jennifer.'

'Well, maybe she did,' said the friend.

'*I* spent the night with Jennifer!'

★ ★ ★

The raddled old prostitute had seen better days.

'Want a good time, dearie?' she asked a passing sailor.

'Well, er, I've only got a fifty pence piece,' he replied quickly.

'That's all right, love,' she assured him. 'I've got change.'

★ ★ ★

The phone rang in the doctor's surgery and a dark brown voice said, 'Doctor, I think you overdid the hormone injections the other day. My voice has gone very deep.'

The doctor replied, 'Don't worry, Miss Wilkinson. It's a perfectly natural reaction. It'll be back to normal in a day or so. By the way, while you're on the phone, are there are any other symptoms?'

'As a matter of fact there are,' said the woman on the other end of the phone. 'I've sprouted thick curly hair in between my breasts.'

'Oh, dear, dear,' said the doctor. 'That's very unusual. Tell me, Miss Wilkinson, how far down does it go?'

'All the way to my testicles!'

★ ★ ★

A rather superior British Army officer spent a very enjoyable night with a high-class prostitute in Hamburg. The next morning he was up bright and early and was just about to sneak through the front door when the prostitute appeared and shouted, 'Not so fast, Englischer swine! What about ze *Marks*?' and she held out her hand.

'Ah yes,' said the officer, bending to kiss her hand. 'Ten out of ten, old girl!'

★ ★ ★

Prostitutes' saying: 'We're in the best business in the world. You got it, you sell it – you *still* got it!'

The young buck went into a large store for a packet of rubbers.

'Have you tried the new rainbow-coloured ones, sir?' asked the assistant. 'We've got blue ones, red ones, green ones . . .'

'I'll try the lot,' said the young man adventurously.

Six months later, he appeared in the same store with a rather sorry-looking young girl asking for a maternity dress.

'What bust, madam?' asked the assistant.

'The *blue* one,' said the young lad sadly.

★   ★   ★

A woman went to see her doctor and explained that she was very worried about becoming pregnant.

'But,' said the doctor, 'I put you on the Pill.'

'Yes, I know,' replied the woman. 'But it keeps on falling out.'

★   ★   ★

A bride who got more than a little drunk at her wedding reception was still determined to say a few words of thanks to the guests for all their presents. She stumbled through a short speech and then slowly turned to point to the presents on display, which included a coffee perculator.

'And finally,' she said, 'I do thank my new parents-in-law for giving me such a beautiful perky copulator.'

★   ★   ★

Flying to a remote part of the world to do missionary work, a plane-load of nuns crashed in a desert. Luckily they all survived, but all their provisions were destroyed, apart from a bag of flour.

Desperately hungry, they searched for water in order to make some bread out of the flour, but to no avail.

'There's only one thing for it,' said the Mother Superior. 'We shall have to make a hole in the ground, fill it with flour and one of you will have to – how shall I say it? – make water into the flour. Needs must.'

So, one by one, the nuns straddled over the flour in the

hole to 'make water', but nerves got the better of them and not one of them was up to the required task, for no matter how hard they tried to force themselves, not one tiny drop was forthcoming.

'It looks as though the Good Lord has chosen me for the task,' said the Mother Superior. 'Make way, and I shall prove equal to it.' The nuns all hid behind bushes to avoid embarrassing the Mother Superior, who squatted over the hole containing the precious flour. But try as she might, the Mother Superior still could not make water, until suddenly, as a result of all the exertion, she let one rip and scattered the flour to the four winds . . . and the nuns all wet themselves laughing!

★   ★   ★

A tourist approached a prostitute in the back streets of Soho.

'How much?' he enquired.

'It'll cost you twenty-five quid, dearie,' replied the tart.

'American Express?' he asked eagerly.

'You can go as fast as you ruddy well like!'

★   ★   ★

Two prostitutes were strolling around London's Piccadilly when one turned to the other and asked, 'Have you ever been picked up by the fuzz?'

'No,' said her friend. 'But I've been swung by the tits a few times.'

★   ★   ★

The novice nun rushed into the Mother Superior's office crying, 'Mother Superior, I've just been raped by a burglar!'

Calmly, the Mother Superior advised the girl to lie down, bite into a lemon, and suck it for half an hour.

'Will that stop me from becoming pregnant?' asked the novice.

'No,' replied the Mother Superior. 'But it'll wipe that ruddy smile off your face.'

★   ★   ★

A worried housewife went to her doctor and showed him some strange small green rings she had developed on the inside of her thighs.

The doctor examined her and announced, 'You've got a gypsy lover!'

'Yes,' gasped the housewife, astounded. 'But how do *you* know?'

'Tell him to take off his earrings next time he comes round,' said the wise old bird.

★   ★   ★

Big Bertha – the striptease artist with the fifty-two inch bust – walked back into the wings after her erotic stage act.

'That was certainly a damned good round of applause you got just now,' said a fellow-stripper.

'That was no applause, darling,' said Bertha. 'That was fly-buttons hitting the ceiling!'

★   ★   ★

'Tell me, how many children have you had, Mrs Fernackapan?' asked the gynaecologist.

'Ten,' she replied.

'Well! One more and you'd have your own football team!' joked the doctor.

'Can't,' said the woman. 'I've no inside-left.'

★   ★   ★

A middle-aged woman got on a London bus trailing three sets of twins. When they were all seated, the conductor couldn't contain his amazement, and asked, 'Do you always get twins?'

'Oh no,' replied the woman, smiling. 'Thousands of times we don't get anything at all!'

★   ★   ★

Man pouring cocktails: 'Say when, dear.'
Girlfriend: 'After the drinks, darling.'

★ ★ ★

A vicar was berating three startled members of his Mothers' Union.

To the first he said, 'You only called your daughter Penny because all you ever thought about was money.' To the second he shouted, 'And *you* called your daughter Sherri because all you ever thought about was drinking.'

The third woman turned to her daughter and said huffily, 'Come on, Fanny. We're not staying here to be insulted!'

★ ★ ★

Husband on his wedding night:
'Oh, darling! That's marvellously tight.'

Wife:
'Take that great hairy thing
out of my navel!'

★ ★ ★

A little girl asked her mother why fairy tales always started 'Once upon a time.'

'They don't *always*,' replied her mother. 'Your father's, for instance, always start "Bloody train was late again tonight".'

★ ★ ★

Two spinsters were sitting at the back of the church one Sunday when, during the sermon, a man sitting in the pew opposite took out his penis and started waving it at them.

One of the spinsters, who had failing eyesight, tried to discern the man and exclaimed, 'Good heavens, Ethel! Is that Dick Green?'

'No,' replied her friend. 'It's just the way the light's shining through the stained-glass window.'

* * *

Two old dears were gossiping in the laundrette.

'The new vicar was giving his first sermon yesterday,' said one.

'Pardon?' said the other, a little hard of hearing.

'I said, the new vicar was giving his first sermon yesterday,' shouted her friend.

'Did he?' came the reply.

'Yes, he bawls like a bull,' said the first.

'Eh?'

'BAWLS LIKE A BULL !' shouted out the friend.

'Has he now!'

Chalkie's little nephew asked him one day, 'Why have I got crinkly black hair?' ''Cos when you're running along in the jungle, it doesn't fall down in front of your eyes like the silly white people's and the sweat doesn't get into your eyes either and make you bump into things,' said Chalkie. 'And why have I got big gangly arms and legs?' asked the nephew. 'And why can I run faster than white people?' 'Well, if the lion's after you in the jungle, you can run like mad and get out of the way,' said Chalkie. 'And why have I got black skin?' 'When the sun's beating down on you you don't blister and burn like the silly white people,' Chalkie told him. 'Why are we living in Balham, then?' asked his nephew.

PRAWN
BALLS

or . . . And Balls to You, Too!

Prawn Balls

I think men must like jokes more than women do and the best jokes, it seems to me, come from Sunday lunchtimes in the pub when the women are at home doing the cooking and the blokes get together having a jar. I used to do a regular Sunday lunchtime spot in the Dun Cow in the Old Kent Road. That was the best time ever for jokes. There was a marvellous atmosphere in there and every joke I ever told seemed funnier there than it did anywhere else in its life. We used to know it by the phrase 'Where there's muck there's money'. I'd go on there and be filthy for a session, and by the time the landlord had called time we'd generally have raised a couple of hundred quid for charity.

Anything to do with sex, or do to with being a failure, will go down well with men. Women tend to laugh at embarrassing situations more than fellows do. Blokes like their jokes to be as broad as possible. They like being put in what you might call a fear situation too; the stories of blokes being caught in bed with another woman have that in them, like the one that comes up in a couple of pages. People say that there are five types of original jokes, but I'm not sure about that. I think there are only two really: laughing at yourself and laughing at other people's misfortunes. And in the case of the humour that appeals to men and the gags about men the biggest laughs always come from the filthiest jokes.

Farmer Giles was walking his donkey to market one day when the animal developed a limp. Dismayed, he knocked on the door of the nearest farmhouse and asked if he could stay the night in order to rest the donkey's legs.

The owner said, 'You can sleep in the spare room upstairs, but the donkey will have to sleep in the shed with the bull.'

They took the donkey into the shed – and there was the bull with the biggest hard-on you've ever seen.

'My God,' said the first farmer. 'Won't it be asking for trouble to leave the donkey with the bull?'

'Not at all,' said the other. 'There's a simple remedy. I'll cover the donkey with this large white blanket and the bull will ignore it and go to sleep.' So the two of them covered up the donkey with the blanket and themselves went to bed.

At about three o'clock in the morning, they were woken by a fearsome commotion coming from the shed, with ear-splitting brayings and the sound of splintering wood. They ran into the shed to find the bull reared up in the corner, still with an enormous hard-on – but no sign of the donkey.

They rushed into the night in pursuit of the donkey, but couldn't find it. Suddenly, rounding a corner, they came across a tramp lying in a hedgerow.

'Hey, you!' shouted one of the farmers. 'Have you by any chance seen a donkey?'

'As a matter of fact, I have,' said the tramp. 'One went past me ten minutes ago, running as if the hounds of hell were after it.'

'Did it have a big white blanket on its back?' asked the farmers.

'Can't say as it had,' said the tramp. 'But it had a little white hanky tucked up its arse.'

★　★　★

An illicit love session was interrupted by the husband's sudden return home.

'Quick – get in the wardrobe!' cried the wife to her frantic lover.

He leaped into the wardrobe but as the woman slammed the door, she trapped his testicles and left them dangling outside.

In strode her suspicious spouse. Spotting the trapped testicles, he shouted, 'What are those?' His wife stammered, 'Er, um, they're a pair of bells I've just bought for my hat.'

'In that case, I'll make the buggers *ring*,' sneered the husband. And he gave them a resounding whack with his rolled umbrella.

There was no sound, so he gave them another swipe. There was still no sound. Striking them again, the husband cried out, 'I still don't hear those bells ringing!' And a muffled voice inside the wardrobe shouted, 'Oh for goodness' sake:

DING BLOODY DONG!'

★ ★ ★

'I can tell it's ages since you've been with a woman,' said the prostitute to her over-active client.

'Well,' smirked the man, 'there's a reason for that. I've been in the VD clinic for six weeks having treatment for syphilis!'

'What's the food like?' asked the prostitute. 'I'm going in tomorrow.'

★ ★ ★

It was the young man's first visit to a prostitute and, after stripping off in the dark, he walked over to her and slipped his willy into her hand. 'What do you think of that?' he asked, proudly.

'Oh, thanks very much,' said the prostitute, feeling at it. 'But if you don't mind I won't smoke it now – I'll slip it behind my ear for later.'

★ ★ ★

Two men were talking in a pub. One said, 'You see my dog here, he's got a degree in metalwork. In fact, believe it or not this dog is a qualified blacksmith.'

'Why, sure he is!' scoffed the other man.

'So you don't believe me, eh?' said the first. 'I'll bet you a fiver.'

'You're on,' said the second man. 'But how are you going to prove it?'

'Watch this,' said the dog's owner. Then he struck a match, held it under the dog's testicles – and the dog made a bolt for the door!

Farmer Giles caught one of his hired hands naked and on the job with his wife. 'Right,' he cried, raising his shotgun. 'I'm going to blow your goolies off!'

'For pity's sake – give me a chance!' pleaded the man.

'All right,' said the farmer, aiming his gun. 'Swing 'em!'

★　★　★

'I have this very personal problem,' mumbled the patient to the doctor.

'I'm a man of the world and you may rely on my discretion completely,' said the doctor reassuringly.

'Well, please do something about this,' muttered the patient. And he took out his willy, which looked like a sawn-off pencil stub no bigger than an inch long.

'Bloody hell!' cried the doctor, bursting into laughter. 'You certainly have a problem there.' And for ten minutes he rolled about on the floor clutching his stomach and laughing uncontrollably until the tears ran down his face. Eventually, he managed to recover his composure.

'I'm so sorry,' he apologised. 'I don't know what came over me. That's the first time I have ever done anything so unprofessional in all my medical life. Now, what seems to be the matter?'

The patient looked at him sadly and said, 'It's swollen.'

★　★　★

> Doctor (on suddenly finding a suppository behind his ear): 'Good heavens! *Now* I remember where I put my pencil!'

★　★　★

A very aristocratic gentleman went to the doctor's and flopped his penis on the doctor's desk.

'I want you to look at that,' he said.

The doctor looked, lifted it and peered at the penis from all angles and then pronounced, 'Well, as far as I can see, there's nothing wrong with that.'

'I know,' said the man proudly. 'It's a *beauty*, isn't it!'

★　★　★

'Doctor, doctor! I've got a bad case of the runs,' said a distraught patient rushing into the surgery.

'When did you first notice this?' asked the doctor.

'When I took my bicycle clips off!'

★　★　★

A worried bachelor went to his doctor when he discovered large red rings all the way round his cock. 'You've got to help me,' he said. 'Can it be cured?'

'Of course it can,' said the doctor. 'Tell your girlfriend to wipe that awful lipstick off first!'

★   ★   ★

Driving up to the old country pub, the director of a major shipping company created quite a stir among the locals with his magnificent yellow Rolls Royce. Just as he was going into the pub, one of the yokels grabbed hold of his arm and asked, 'Excuse me asking, but 'ow can 'ee afford a bootiful car like that?'

Haughtily the director raised himself to his full height, looked down his nose with some distaste at the rustic and explained, 'My good man, I work f'Cunnard.'

The yokel scratched his head, stared back at the man and declared, 'Arr, an' *I* works f'kin 'ard too, but *I* can't afford a car like that!'

★   ★   ★

A man went into a chemist's and asked the assistant for some deodorant.

'Ball or aerosol?' asked the assistant.

'Neither, it's for under me *arms*,' replied the customer.

★   ★   ★

An old man was standing in the gents with tears streaming down his face.

'Whatever's the matter?' asked the man standing next to him.

'Look at it!' exclaimed the old man. 'It used to be fifteen inches and one wrinkle – now it's fifteen wrinkles and one inch!'

★   ★   ★

Into a crowded pub staggered a man with two wooden legs. Tottering precariously up to the bar, he ordered a pint of best bitter.

'I'll make that right,' said the landlord.

'Look,' snapped the man. 'Just because I've got two wooden legs doesn't mean I'm incapable of buying my own beer.' And he slammed the money down on the bar and

59

started his pint.

Later that night, he asked the landlord where the gents was.

'Through the back door and down the yard,' said the landlord. 'But it's been snowing, and the yard is cobbled so it could be a bit slippery. I'll take you down.'

'I've told you,' shouted the man. 'I may have two wooden legs but I can still look after myself. Leave me alone!' And he clomped off outside.

Half an hour later, the landlord realised the man hadn't returned and he was about to go outside to look for him when the door burst open and in staggered the man with his shirt ripped up the back, his hair full of snow and covered from head to foot in muck.

'What did I tell you,' said the landlord. 'I did warn you about the slippery cobblestones!'

'Cobblestones be damned!' raged the man. 'I was sat on the toilet, minding my own business, when some silly bugger flung the door open, grabbed hold of my wooden legs and yanked me out, saying, "Who's left this ruddy wheelbarrow in here?"'

★ ★ ★

The elephant and the snake were walking through the jungle.

'I'm bored,' complained the snake. 'I wish we had some games to play.'

'Fancy a game of snooker?' asked the elephant.

'I'd love one,' replied the snake. 'But we don't have a snooker table.'

'That doesn't matter, we'll improvise!' said the elephant. 'We'll do little tricks, and award each other points. I'll go first.' And he slowly balanced on his front legs and walked round the snake.

'That's very good,' said the snake. 'I'll award you a blue for that. Now watch me.' And he stood up straight on the end of his tail, flipped in the air and did a somersault.

'Marvellous!' said the elephant. 'I'll award you a pink for that. Now it's my turn again.' And he balanced on the end of his trunk with all four legs in the air.

'Superb!' cried the snake. 'I'll give you the black for that. I can't beat you – you're too good.'

'I'll tell you what,' said the elephant. 'If you can crawl up my bottom, through my insides and out through my trunk, that'll be a fantastic trick, and I'll give you the game.'

'What a good idea!' said the snake excitedly. 'I'll give it a try.' And the snake crawled up the elephant's bottom and disappeared out of sight.

Suddenly the elephant took his trunk, pushed it up his own bottom and with a muffled cry of elation shouted: 'Ha-Ha! You're snookered!'

★　★　★

Pansy Pete was mincing into the pub one evening when he slipped in a huge pile of dog muck on the doorstep, did a double somersault and landed in the pile with his suit in a mess. He rushed off to the gents to clean up, and came back into the pub to see a huge Irish navvy slip in the same pile and slide along the floor of the pub with his head banging into the bar.

'Oh!' said Pansy Pete, rushing over to him. '*I've* just done that!'

'You filthy sod!' exclaimed the navvy, and rubbed his nose in it.

★　★　★

A little old man of eighty-nine asked the doctor, 'Is it possible to have a transplant at my age?' to which the doctor replied, 'Transplant? What sort of transplant had you in mind?'

The old man said, 'Well, you see, what happened was . . . I had it shot off in the Great War. You know, my *thingy*!'

The doctor said, 'Yes, I know. I have your file here. What about it?'

'Well, I want to know if I can have it sewn back on. You see, when it was shot off, my mate Charlie put it in my tobacco tin for me, and what with all these medical advances like transplants and whatnot, I wondered if it would be possible to have it stitched back on again.'

The doctor was aghast. 'But the war was over sixty years

ago! Can you imagine what condition your severed penis will be in?'

'Have a look for yourself,' said the old man. 'I've brought it to show you.' And he handed the doctor the old tobacco tin.

Very carefully, the doctor opened the rusty old tin, took out the object lying there with a pair of tweezers and examined it closely under a magnifying glass. He looked more closely, sniffed it once or twice, and turned to the old man, 'Do you know what this it?'

'I've told you,' said the old man getting agitated. 'It's what I had shot off in the war!'

'My dear fellow,' said the doctor, '*this* is the butt end of a Wills Whiff cigar!'

The old man sat there with tears coming to his eyes and said, 'Oh, bloody hell! *I've smoked me willy!*'

★   ★   ★

A rabbi and a priest were travelling together on a train.

After a while, the rabbi turned to the priest and remarked, 'One thing has always puzzled me. Why do you wear your collar back to front?'

The priest replied, 'That's because I'm a father.'

The rabbi said, 'I'm a father too – I have three wonderful sons!'

'You misunderstood me,' said the priest, smiling. 'I'm a father of 5,000.'

'You dirty beggar!' exclaimed the rabbi. 'It's your *trousers* you should wear back to front, not your collar!'

★   ★   ★

An Irishman was walking a giraffe on a lead down the main shopping street when he was stopped by a policeman.

'What are you doing with that giraffe?' asked the bobby

'I'm taking it to be mated, sorr,' replied the Irishman.

'Where?' asked the bobby in amazement. The Irishman went round to the back of the giraffe, lifted up its tail and pointed, 'THERE!'

★   ★   ★

— THERE!

Walking into the gents of his local, Norman noticed a man standing with his legs crossed and his hands held out in front of him, shaking so hard that his fingers were nearly dropping off.

'Please help me,' said the man, still shaking pitifully. 'Would you do me the kindness of unzipping my fly?'

Feeling sorry for the obviously seriously afflicted fellow, Norman obliged, albeit somewhat embarrassed.

'Take it out and hold it while I pee, would you, please?' asked the man, shaking even more violently.

Feeling highly uncomfortable, but being a helpful sort of chap, Norman duly obliged him.

'Now shake the drops off for me, would you?' said the man.

Again Norman obliged.

'And would you tuck it back in and zip me up, please?' asked the man.

So Norman did as he was asked and then led the man out of the gents to his seat at the bar. Suddenly his curiosity got the better of him and pointing at the man's shaking hands, he asked timidly, 'Excuse me asking, but is it shell-shock?'

'Heavens no, ducky!' exclaimed the man. 'I'm just drying my nail varnish!'

★　★　★

What do you call a queer at a christening?
　　A fairy godfather.

★　★　★

The crowded bus pulled up at the request stop and a large sweaty fat man struggled to heave a big trunk on to the platform.

'I'm sorry, sir,' said the conductor. 'This bus is full – you can't come on here with that trunk!'

Angrily the man dragged the trunk off the platform, shouting, 'You can stuff the bus up your backside!' To which the conductor retorted, 'And if *you* could do the same with that trunk you'd be able to get on the bloody bus!'

★　★　★

Overheard on Inter-city train:
Passenger to steward: 'This tea tastes like cat's piss.'
Steward to passenger: 'Pardon me, sir. That's coffee.
The tea tastes like camel dung!'

★   ★   ★

Which reminds me of how careful you should be when pouring drinks for your girlfriend – she may be after gin and platonic, when what you're hoping for is whisky and sofa!

★   ★   ★

The Protestant-turned-Catholic was in the confession box for the first time and he was admitting to the sin of adultery.
'How many times, my son?' asked the priest.
'Blimey!' said the man, 'I didn't come here to *brag* about it!'

★   ★   ★

An American was going on his first business trip to Tokyo and a friend gave him some advice.
'Hank,' said the friend, 'when you get over there, you must go with one of those lovely geisha girls. They can do things you ain't *dreamed* of in your wildest fantasies! And whatever you do, don't forget to ask for the Wax Treatment!'
'The Wax Treatment?' said Hank. 'What in tarnation is the Wax Treatment!'
'You'll find out!' said the friend, chuckling.
The following week in Tokyo, Hank followed his friend's advice and paid a visit to a geisha girl – a beautiful dark-eyed creature who ministered to his every whim. She massaged him with her feet, her breasts, in fact with every part of her delicious young body.
'Well now, little lady,' said Hank, 'this is all well and good. But what I *really* want is the Wax Treatment.'
'The Wax Treatment is *very* expensive,' replied the girl. 'Plenty dollar to pay.'
'I don't care how much it costs,' replied Hank. 'The Wax

Treatment I want, and the Wax Treatment I shall have!'
And he handed over the contents of his wallet.

'Lie back, then, and close your eyes,' said the geisha girl.
'Are you comfortable? Then open your legs,' she went on.
As Hank murmured contentedly, she leant underneath the
bed and drew out a massive pair of silver cymbals.

'You ready now for Wax Treatment?' she asked huskily.

'Sure am!' said Hank. So the girl brought the cymbals
together with an almighty crash on his cobblers – and the
wax shot out of his ears!

★   ★   ★

A martial arts fanatic travelled thousands of miles to meet
with the greatest living karate expert – a wizened old man
living in a yak-hide tent in the foothills of the Himalayas.

Approaching him reverently, he asked the old man if he
would consent to show him just one example of his
prowess. The old man nodded silently and, spying a fly
coming through the tent-flap, he raised his hand and with
the speed of light chopped down and took off the fly's left
wing, which spiralled down to the floor.

'Unbelievable!' said the adherent excitedly. 'Master,
would you show me something else?'

The old man nodded again, and as another fly flew by
him, he brought down his hand and took off its right wing.

'Master, your skill astounds me,' cried the man. 'Please,
I beg of you, show me just one more example of your
dexterity and I shall go home a happy man.'

Sighing deeply, the old man agreed to the importunate
fanatic's request. As a third fly entered the tent, he
whipped out the side of his hand at it – but to his pupil's
amazement, it sailed by unconcernedly and went back out
through the tent-flap.

'Huh!' cried the visitor. 'You didn't even *hit* that fly!
You're no expert after all!'

The old man simply opened his hand and showed the
fanatic two tiny black specks in the middle of his palm. 'My
son,' he said quietly, 'that fly will never be a father again.'

★   ★   ★

A sewage farm worker was filling in his census form, and under 'Occupation' he wrote down 'crap-shoveller'. When the local census inspector saw the offending words he paid a visit to the man.

'What on earth do you mean by putting "crap-shoveller" down on your census return?' he ranted. 'There are girls in our office and they were very upset by your thoughtless choice of words. Why couldn't you have written down "excreta excavator" instead?'

'If I could spell "excreta excavator",' replied the man, 'I wouldn't be a bloody crap-shoveller, would I?'

★ ★ ★

Chatting sociably to the pub landlord, a passing customer noticed out of the corner of his eye that the landlord's rather large alsation was lying on the carpet licking its testicles.

Winking at the landlord, the customer said, rather humorously, 'I wish *I* could do that . . .'

'Well, give him a biscuit and he might let you,' replied the landlord.

★ ★ ★

Why was the Grand Old Duke of York the biggest fairy of all times?

Because he had Ten Thousand Men.

★ ★ ★

Meeting an old friend who he hadn't seen for many years, Jack invited him back to his home to stay the night.

'I'm afraid you'll have to sleep in the same bedroom as my brother-in-law who's staying with us,' said Jack. 'And I must warn you that he snores like a machine-gun – you might not get much shut-eye!'

'Don't worry,' said the friend. 'I'll sleep all right!'

The next morning Jack was surprised to find his old friend full of the joys of spring and whistling like a skylark. He told Jack he had slept like a log.

'But how did you manage to, with all that snoring?' asked Jack.

'Well, before your brother-in-law got into bed I kissed him on the cheek and patted his bum – and *he* never slept a wink all night!'

* ★ ★

Enoch Powell died and went to Heaven. He came to the Pearly Gates and knocked.

'Who dat dere?' boomed a voice.

And Enoch said, 'Oh *balls*!' and walked down the staircase.

* ★ ★

Two jet pilots crashed in the jungle and were captured by cannibals who put them in a large pot full of boiling water. Suddenly one of the pilots burst out laughing at the top of his voice.

'What the hell is there to laugh about at a time like this?' asked the other.

'I've just done something in their stew!' replied the other.

* ★ ★

Chinless Wonder found himself standing at the side of a large coloured man at the bar of a pub.

'I say, you dark chappies are supposed to be well hung, eh? What? I hope you don't mind me asking, old man, but exactly how long is it?'

'Three inches,' replied the man.

'Haw-haw!' chortled Chinless. 'I say, that's not very big, is it!'

'That's three inches *off the floor*,' came the cool reply.

* ★ ★

Two gays went on a holiday cruise together, but during a heavy swell, one fell overboard.

'Help!' he shouted. 'Throw me a buoy!'

'That's my Cecil!' said his friend proudly. 'Game to the last!'

* ★ ★

Have you ever heard of Bernard the Brown-nosed
    Reindeer?
No?
Well, he's the one who stands behind Rudolph – but he
    can't stop as fast.

★   ★   ★

The panda-car policeman stopped the sports-car freak for
speeding.
    'Name?'
    'Percy Pimpleprick,' replied the man, at which the
bobby burst into fits of laughter.
    'Excuse me, sir, but that really is a very funny name,' he
said.
    'Actually,' said the young man huffily, 'I think Percy's
quite a nice name myself!'

★   ★   ★

Porky the pig walked into his local and downed thirty pints
of best bitter. On his way home, he stopped for a pee in one
shop doorway after another and was soon apprehended by a
policeman.

'Hello, 'ello, 'ello,' said the bobby
'And I suppose you're the little
piggy who went to market?'
'No,' replied Porky.
'*I'm* the little piggy who went wee,
wee, wee, all the way home.'

An Irishman came over to England and went down to Murphy's where only Irish people were employed, and was given a job. 'What about digs?' he asked and they told him to go to Mrs Scrubit's down the road, where all the other workers lived. Mrs Scrubit had only one bed left, because she took in black lodgers as well, and the Irishman had to share a room with Chalkie. They got talking, then went out for a drink with all the other Irish lads and the blacks. As they were leaving, the Irishman asked Mrs Scrubit to be sure to wake him at seven o'clock to start his new job the next day. At the end of a very good evening the Irishman had to be carried home and, for a joke, Chalkie got some boot polish and blacked his face up. Unfortunately neither of them heard Mrs Scrubit's knock the next morning and at nine-thirty she came in telling Paddy to get up because he was late. So he threw on his donkey jacket and wellington boots over his pyjamas and ran down to Murphy's yard. But the man on the gate wouldn't let him in. 'I've come for the new job,' he protested. 'I'm sorry, mate, there's only Irish people taken on here,' the man explained. 'What are you talking about?' asked Paddy, 'I'm from Dublin.' 'Well, you'd better go in the office and wait,' the gateman told him. While he was sitting in the boss's office he looked in a mirror on the wall, saw his face all blacked up and said, 'Saints alive! The stupid woman's woken the wrong one.'

CHOP SUEY

or Marital and Extra-marital Magic

Chop Suey

Wedding jokes and jokes about honeymoons have a humour based on the anticipation and nervousness that builds up to a peak before it becomes a terrible letdown. You can also walk on stage and say 'I'm a married man', which will always raise a laugh. Together they form the basis of one of the most popular types of joke for both men and women. Honeymoon jokes in particular offer all the staple ingredients of a successful adult joke: sex, laughing at other people's misfortunes and the thought that there but for the grace of God go I.

One that I tell deals with the poor girl who lost a leg in an accident. Whenever a boyfriend found out she had a false leg, he'd leave her, so she decided not to tell the next one. After going out with a really nice fellow for some time, without having any sex, they got married and found themselves in their honeymoon room. The bride took off her false leg and put it on the mantelpiece before her husband came out of the bathroom. When he joined her in bed he ran his hand up her real leg but couldn't find her other one. 'Where's your leg?' he asked. 'It's on the mantelpiece,' she told him. 'Well, there's no need to open them that wide, darling,' he said.

Jokes about marriage are a natural lead on to embarrassing situations that occur outside it in every respect, so in this 'chop suey' you'll find a mixture of jokes about married people from inside and outside their 'connubial bliss.'

A newly-married couple were spending their honeymoon at home and all their efforts at love-making were ending in frustration.

'It's simply too big for me, darling,' said the young wife. 'You'll have to go downstairs for some Vaseline!'

Foaming at the mouth, her husband ran downstairs three

steps at a time with the most enormous erection standing out like a flagpole. As he burst into the kitchen, the dog shot under the table, the cat jumped out of the window and the parrot stood on one leg, tucked its wing up under its armpit and screeched, 'You wouldn't rape a cripple would yer?'

★   ★   ★

A married couple were standing outside the ape-house at the local zoo and the wife was sneeringly making comparisons between the gorilla's courting tackle and that of her henpecked husband. Suddenly, the gorilla grabbed hold of her, pulled her through the bars and started to make mad, passionate love to her.

'Help! Charlie! What should I do?' screamed the wife.

'Do what you always do,' answered her husband. 'Tell him you've got a headache!'

★   ★   ★

Does your new film role give you lots of lines?'
'Not really. I'm playing the husband.'

★   ★   ★

An eighty-year-old man who married a seventeen-year-old girl went to his doctor to seek his advice.

'What's the trouble?' asked the doctor.

'Well, you see, it's like this,' said the old man. 'I'd like us to have children, but I'm concerned about the difference in our ages.'

'No problem,' said the medical man. 'Why don't you get a lodger younger than yourself?' he suggested, with a wink and a nudge.

'Thanks!' said the old man. 'I never thought of that.'

Some months later, the two met again.

'How's the wife?' asked the doctor.

'Great – she's expecting twins in a few months,' answered the old man proudly.

'Ah,' replied the doctor, 'I see you took a lodger like I suggested?'

'That's right!' said the old man gleefully. 'And *she's* in the pudding club too!'

★ ★ ★

Their sex life was non-existent and as the wife took off her clothes in the bedroom, her husband glanced at her pubic region and said, 'Good heavens, Nellie! You're going grey down there!'

'Grey be damned!' moaned the wife. 'Those are *cobwebs*!'

★ ★ ★

Jack went home on his fifth wedding anniversary and presented his wife with a large bunch of flowers.

'I suppose I've got to open my legs for these, have I?' she snarled.

'Why?' replied Jack. 'Haven't you got a vase large enough?'

★ ★ ★

The cuckolded husband arrived home unexpectedly and found his wife lying naked in bed and a big fat cigar smouldering in the ashtray. With a voice like thunder, he exploded, 'And where the hell did that cigar come from?' And a nervous voice from inside the wardrobe answered, 'Havana.'

★ ★ ★

'I'm getting really worried,' said a man to his doctor. 'Whenever I go on the lavatory, it comes out like chips.'

'Just a minute, I know how to cure this,' said the doctor. He disappeared for a few moments and emerged from the waiting room with a huge pair of gleaming garden shears. 'Drop your trousers, would you?' he asked.

'What the hell are you going to do with those?' asked the patient nervously.

'I'm going to cut six inches off the bottom of your string vest!'

★ ★ ★

Stripped off and admiring himself in the bedroom mirror, Mr Wonderful turned to his wife and said, 'Look at that physique! It's *dynamite*!'

'Yes,' she replied sadly. 'It's a pity it has such a short fuse.'

* * *

OH YES, YOUR BODY'S DYNAMITE—
IT'S SUCH A PITY IT HAS SUCH A
SHORT FUSE...

A bridegroom-to-be asked his best man if there was any sure way he could find out if his future wife had been with any other men.

'Simple!' said his friend. 'All you have to do is take a pot of green paint, a pot of purple paint and a shovel on your honeymoon.'

'Whatever for?' asked the bridegroom in amazement. 'How will that prove anything?'

'Well,' said the best man. 'You paint your left testicle green, the right one purple. And if she says, "I've never seen a pair of green and purple balls before!" you hit her over the head with the shovel!'

★　★　★

At the end of a company board meeting, the chairman concluded, 'And I'd like to know who has been fooling around with my secretary.'

No one responded, and there was nervous shuffling and muttering around the table.

'All right,' said the chairman, 'who has *not* been fooling around with my secretary?'

After a brief silence, one man coughed hesitantly and said, 'Me, sir.'

The chairman glared, and then said, 'Right. *You* fire her!'

★　★　★

After a hectic few hours' love-making with his gorgeous blonde secretary one evening, the businessman got out of bed and dressed. Then he spilled cigarette ash down the front of his suit, dabbed some whisky behind each ear and covered his lapels with billiard chalk.

When he got home bleary-eyed, his wife was waiting for him with a menacing gleam in her eye.

'And where the hell have *you* been till this time of night?' she demanded.

'Where d'you think – I've been screwing my secretary,' he told her.

'I wasn't bloody born yesterday!' his wife bawled. 'Look at the state of you! You've been down that bloody club again playing snooker!'

★　★　★

Nervously, a young nurse approached a big Irishman in the
maternity wing. 'Excuse me, Mr O'Riley,' she squeaked.
'I'm happy to tell you your baby has arrived . . . only . . .
I'm afraid to have to tell you . . . it's, er, black.'

'Jasus!' exclaimed O'Riley. 'That'll be the wife's fault!
She burns absolutely bloody everything!'

★　★　★

Passengers in a first-class railway compartment looked on in
horror as the man in bowler hat and pinstriped suit took
down his trousers, removed his hat, and began to defecate
into it. When he had finished, cool as a cucumber he took
the hat and threw its steaming contents through the
window and resumed his seat.

Stunned into a more deafening silence than usual, the
other occupants nervously shuffled their feet, with the
exception of one man who took out a large cigar and started
to smoke it in order to mask the unholy smell that was
permeating through the compartment. At which the man in
the bowler hat looked up from his *Financial Times*, calmly
tapped the man on the shoulder, and said, 'I say, old boy,
play the game! It *is* a non-smoker, you know!'

★　★　★

A policeman caught a man behind a hedge, masturbating
into a five-pound note.

'And what's *your* game, then?' he boomed.

'I've just come into money,' replied the man.

★　★　★

Early one morning, a young holiday couple were met out in
the fields by an old farmer who politely enquired if they
were enjoying their stay in the country.

'It's wonderful, thank you,' said the girl. 'We've been up
bright and early collecting frogsdicks.'

'Frogsdicks?' gasped the old farmer, his pipe dropping
from his mouth in amazement.

'She means *toadstools*,' said the young man sheepishly.

*   *   *

A poor man had a painfully small penis and volunteered to become the world's first penis transplant recipient. A donor had to be found, however, and as not many men were keen on the idea of donating their courting tackle, the doctors decided to go round to the local zoo and take one off the gorilla. The operation was carried out and pronounced a success.

A year later, thanks to his newly-acquired willy, the man was in the maternity hospital waiting excitedly for his wife to give birth to their first child. The nurse rushed up to him and gasped, 'Congratulations! You're the father of triplets!'

'Triplets!' exclaimed the man. 'Well! What sex are they?'

'We don't know,' said the nurse. 'They're still swinging round the bedposts.'

*   *   *

'Doctor,' said a man frantically. 'I think I'm going round the bend. I feel so run down, and it's because I can't stop eating snooker balls!'

'Good heavens!' cried the horrified physician. 'How many a day do you actually eat?'

'Well, take today for example. I had three reds for breakfast, followed by a blue for elevenses, some reds and a yellow for lunch and a pink during tea break. Then I had four reds, a black and the white for dinner.'

'A-ha,' said the doctor. 'The cause of your trouble is obvious. 'You're not getting enough *greens* down you.'

*   *   *

Harry confided to his best friend Jack that he'd caught a dose of crabs, and asked his advice on the best means of removing them.

'Do what I used to do when I was in the army,' advised Jack. 'Before you go to bed tonight, rub a pound-and-a-half of sugar all over your balls.'

'And will that shift the little so-and-so's?' asked Harry incredulously.

'No,' replied Jack. 'But it will rot their teeth and stop the little buggers biting!'

* * *

Coming home from work unexpectedly, Big Mick the Irish navvy caught the doctor having sex with his wife on the sofa. Startled but quick-thinking, the doctor tried to reassure him by saying, 'It's OK. I'm just taking your wife's temperature.'

'Is dat so!' said Mick slowly. 'Well, dat ting had better have bloody *numbers* on it when you pull it out!'

* * *

Mr and Mrs Smith had a very unsatisfactory love life and, just for a joke, Mr Smith presented his wife with a tombstone, while she was still alive, and on it he had inscribed the epitaph:

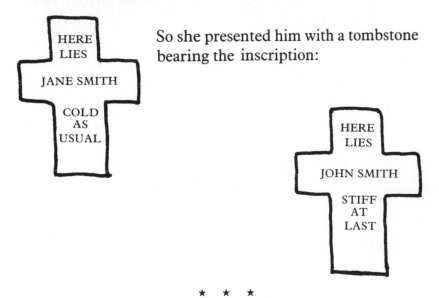

So she presented him with a tombstone bearing the inscription:

HERE
LIES

JANE SMITH

COLD
AS
USUAL

HERE
LIES

JOHN SMITH

STIFF
AT
LAST

* * *

Hearing loud, agonised screams coming from the outpatients' department, a doctor rushed in and yelled at a student nurse, 'For goodness' sake, nurse! I said prick his *boils*!'

* * *

Devilish Derek slipped his oversized tool into the hand of an inexperienced young thing.

'Oo-oo, and what do you call this?' she exclaimed.

'Kipling,' growled the cad.

'What a funny name. Why do you call it that?'

'Cos it's *ruddyard*,' he replied.

★ ★ ★

'It's my sex-maniac husband,' said an anxious women to her doctor. 'He keeps sucking my left nipple in bed. He won't leave it alone. What can I do?'

'I know what will cure him,' said the doctor, smiling. 'Smear your breast with the strongest-smelling Lymeswold you can get.'

Next week, the woman arrived at the surgery nursing a swollen nipple.

'What's the matter – didn't the cheese cure him?' asked the doctor.

'Did it hell,' replied the woman. 'He comes to bed with a big jar of pickled onions every night now!'

★ ★ ★

A woman had given birth to fifteen children and was lying on a doctor's couch with her legs wide open while the doctor made a close inspection. Sadly he shook his head and said, 'I'm afraid you can't have any more children, Mrs Flanagan. I'm afraid you can't have any more children, Mrs Flanagan.'

'I'm not deaf,' snapped the woman. 'You don't need to repeat yourself!'

'I didn't,' said the doctor. 'That was the echo.'

★ ★ ★

A young, engaged couple were having sex on the canal bank when the girl asked sweetly, 'Syd, darling, when we have a baby boy, what shall we call him?' Callously, Syd tied a knot in the condom, threw it in the canal and announced, 'If he gets out of *that*, we'll call him Houdini!'

★ ★ ★

An old man of ninety-two had taken a bride of sixteen, and his doctor was advising him . . .

'Look,' said the doctor, 'if you have sex, it could prove fatal.'

'If she dies, she dies!' said the old man.

★　★　★

He: 'Let's make love a different way tonight, darling!'
She: 'How?'
He: 'Let's do it back to back.'
She: 'Don't be silly – you can't make love back to back.'
He: 'Oh yes you can!'
She: 'How?'
He: 'I've invited another couple.'

★　★　★

Two old friends met after a long time apart: 'How many kids have you got now, Bill?' asked one.

'Ten,' said Bill. 'All boys.'

'Well! One more and you'd have your own football team,' laughed his friend.

'And how many children have you got?' asked Bill.

'Seventeen,' said his friend. 'All girls.'

'One more and you'd have your own golf course!'

★　★　★

A soccer player was unable to fulfil his connubial obligations, due to concentrating too much on football and not enough on his wife. In desperation, she went to the doctor and asked him to give her something to remedy the situation, and make her husband more virile.

'Slip a couple of these into his tea and everything will be OK,' the doctor guaranteed, and he handed her a bottle of pills.

When she got home, the wife duly put the pills in her husband's tea and within fifteen minutes he jumped up, stripped all his clothes off and yelled, 'Go upstairs this minute and take off that basque!'

Overjoyed, his wife did as she was told, and lay naked and expectant on the bed. Suddenly, the door burst open and in walked her husband in his football kit.

'What's the idea?' asked the wife.

'I feel so good that I'm going to get the lads together for a game of football,' replied her husband.

'Why the hell did you want me to take off my basque, then?'

'Because I need the laces for my boots,' he replied.

★ ★ ★

The bored sophisticate went into a house of ill repute in Soho and asked for 'something really different'. He was shown to a room on the top floor where he was stripped and tied to a naked woman and hung upside-down outside the window by a chain on the end of a crane.

Just as the couple were getting it together, the chain snapped and they crashed to the pavement in the street below. A passing Irishman rushed up to the door of the brothel, rang the bell, banged on the door, and shouted through the letterbox, 'Excuse me, but your sign's just fallen off!'

★ ★ ★

On to the shop-floor walked Bert with a black eye, broken nose and busted lip. His workmates asked him how he came to have them.

'It's like this,' he explained. 'The blonde bird next door invited me in for a cup of tea and a chat – purely platonic, you understand! Not wishing to seem unneighbourly, of course, I said yes. I was drinking the tea when she noticed that I had a button missing off my fly, and she offered to sew one of her husband's on for me. Of course, I was a bit embarrassed, but she said I could leave the trousers on. And she did sew the button on. That's how I got my injuries.'

'But what do you mean?' asked his puzzled workmates.

'She was bending down to bite the cotton thread off the fly button when her bloody husband walked in!'

★ ★ ★

A farmer was taking a sample of his wife's urine to the

pregnancy testing clinic but, unbeknown to him, his friends had exchanged his wife's sample for that of the old sow's.

The doctor took the sample to the laboratory for examination, and came back a few minutes later to announce to the startled farmer, 'You're going to be the father of a healthy baby piglet!'

Indignantly, the farmer flopped his penis on the doctor's desk and shouted, 'Oh yes! And what do you think *this* is? A bloody pork sausage?'

★   ★   ★

Keith and his wife were enjoying a meal in their favourite restaurant and she was proudly displaying her new low-cut evening gown. Suddenly, she clutched her chest and yelled, 'I've got heartburn!'

'Don't be stupid,' replied Keith calmly. 'Your left tit's dangling in the ashtray!'

★   ★   ★

Two friends were chatting in a pub. One said, 'I say, Charlie, do you like scabby old women with big floppy tits, flabby bums and large hairy wotnots?'

'Of course not!' retorted Charlie.

'Then leave my wife alone!' said his friend.

★   ★   ★

> **She was only the architect's daughter – but she let the borough surveyor.**

★   ★   ★

On Randy Andy's first day at a nudist camp the lecherous swine 'accidentally' bumped into the camp beauty – a voluptuous seventeen-year-old blonde.

'Oops! Sorry, miss,' he apologised. 'The old headlamps aren't working too well,' he said, pointing to his eyes.

'No,' she replied, 'but there's nothing wrong with your indicator, is there?'

★　★　★

Soldiers on manoeuvres in the Lake District noticed that some equipment was missing. They told the platoon leader, who got on a crackling phone line to GHQ and said, 'Send us three punts and a canoe right away.'

The following morning he got a telegram: 'Girls on way. But what the hell's a panoe?'

★　★　★

Cycling down to work one day, the chain came off Chalkie's bike and while he was struggling to get it back on a bloke pulled up in an E-Type Jag and asked, 'Have you broken down?' Chalkie said he had. 'Well, can I give you a lift?' 'No, sir,' said Chalkie, 'I can't leave my bike here.' 'Well, can I give you a tow?' and he gave Chalkie a rope to tie round his handle-bars. 'If I go too fast, you just ring the bell and I'll slow down,' the driver said as he started up. At first all was going well. The driver kept his speed to a sedate fifteen miles an hour and Chalkie had his feet up on the handle-bars enjoying his ride. Then a bloke in a Jensen shot past, doing about ninety. The E-type driver wasn't having any of that and set off after him, completely forgetting about Chalkie. Further down the road they roared past a policeman who grabbed his radio and reported, 'I've just seen a Jensen Interceptor doing about 110 mph, followed by an E-type Jaguar doing 130 mph, followed by a big black man on his push bike ringing his bell and trying to pass both of them.'

SPECIAL FRIED RICE

or Pot Luck

Special Fried Rice

Although I've tried to classify the jokes in the earlier sections, one of the secrets of being a successful comedian, I'm sure, is being able to adapt your material – being able to call on jokes about all sorts of different things. That's why the ones that follow are a general collection covering lots of different topics.

When I got started I used to write the tag lines of each of my jokes in a book. It was a small book, about four inches square, like a little address book. I had a thousand in there by the time I'd finished and then I lost it – in the Dun Cow public house in the Old Kent Road, in 1976. If anyone ever found that little black book, can I have it back? It won't mean anything to anyone else, and I know most of the jokes by heart now, but I'd love to have it for old time's sake.

Of course I don't use all my jokes at the same time. I keep some in reserve, giving them a break, before bringing them back for another airing. That's why having a book can be useful, especially if your memory isn't all that it might be. That's also why it's useful to have a wide range of material – in case you find you've forgotten a few.

Did you hear the one about . . .

the constipated alcoholic who couldn't pass a pub?

the man who was so unlucky that at his grandfather's cremation he got a cinder in his eye?

the woman who was so ugly as a kid that dirty old men used to give her sweets to get out of their cars?

the dirty old flea-circus owner who invited a girl back to his tent to show her his itchings?'

the very elderly gentleman who invited a pretty young girl upstairs to see him make his will?

the Scottish angler who married a girl with worms?

the girl who was so dim she had to take off her bra to count to two?

the two sex-mad worms who were caught making love in the graveyard in dead Ernest?

the Irish fellow who stayed up all night studying for a urine test?

the flasher who, on cold nights, used to leap out at women and *describe* himself?

Walking down the street, the young schoolgirl found her path blocked by a golden ladder which appeared to have grown out of the pavement and extended upwards, bearing the legend:

CLIMB THE LADDER TO SUCCESS!

Intrigued by the message, she started to climb up the ladder, and halfway up was another message, saying:

KEEP CLIMBING THE LADDER TO SUCCESS!

After half an hour she was still climbing. About to give up, she eventually arrived at the top of the ladder – and there to her horror sat a large black man with an enormous tool in his hand.

'Who are you?' she cried out in fear.

'I'SE CESS!' he whooped happily.

★   ★   ★

A young girl was making sure of a young man's intentions before agreeing to go out with him.

'If we go out for a drive, there'll be no kissing and

cuddling? No running out of petrol?' she asked.

'No, of course not!' he replied.

'And if we go to your flat, will you be good?'

'Yes, I will.'

'Well then,' she sighed, 'there's not much fun in going out with you, is there!'

★ ★ ★

When I was only a young lad, I saw this beautiful girl, and I threw her down on the grass, flung her skirt over her head, tore off her tights, and attacked her panties . . . I needed the elastic for my catapult!

★ ★ ★

> **Did you hear about the gamekeeper who saw a naked young woman in the woods and asked if she was game? When she said yes, he shot her.**

★ ★ ★

I wonder if the Scots really are as mean as they're supposed to be? Judge for yourselves.

You know you're at a Scottish wedding when the confetti is all on elastic. The Scots are the only people in the world who go into a neighbour's house, to use their gas to commit suicide. And what do you suppose happens if you put a goat in a Scotsman's garden? He doesn't complain that the goat is eating all his plants – he gets a bucket and milks it!

★ ★ ★

Why is marriage like a three-ring circus?

First, there's the engagement ring; second, there's the wedding ring; third, there's the suffering.

★ ★ ★

What's the difference between knowledge and faith?

Well, a mother knows that her children are hers – a father believes that his children are his.

★ ★ ★

During the Second World War Private Jenkins served under a particularly objectionable Colonel, Colonel Bagshawe. Bagshawe seemed to do everything possible to be horrible to his men, and they all hated him.

After the war was over, Jenkins went into business and did quite well for himself. He gradually got richer and climbed up the social ladder, spending his spare time playing golf with other rich businessmen. One of them persuaded him to join a particularly posh club, and though Jenkins wasn't keen he allowed himself to be persuaded.

On his first evening there, however, he felt that his misgivings had been well founded. The first person he came face to face with was Bagshawe.

'Hello there, Jenkins,' sneered Bagshawe. 'What are you doing here?'

'Hello, sir. I've just joined,' replied Jenkins.

'Really?' The colonel looked surprised. 'And are you a town member or a country member?'

'A town member, sir,' replied Jenkins.

'*I'm* a country member,' said Bagshawe grandly.

'Yes, sir, I remember,' said Jenkins.

★ ★ ★

A doddering old English aristocrat met a woman who was only marginally younger than himself at a garden party. Fancying his chances, he asked her if he could take her home.

'Yes,' replied the old dear. 'But I must warn you that I'm in the menopause.'

'That's quite all right, m'dear,' said the old buffer. 'You lead off and I'll follow you in the Rolls.'

★ ★ ★

A bill-poster was putting up a life-sized poster outside a theatre advertising a forthcoming pop concert. A young girl with pebble-lens glasses gazed up at the poster and asked, 'Excuse me, mister – is Cliff Richard coming?'

'Is he, heck!' exclaimed the bill-poster. 'It's just a bit of paste off the end of me brush.'

The new secretary at the office was finding her bearings.

'Excuse me,' she said nervously, approaching the boss. 'Do you use Dictaphone?'

'No, of course not!' he snapped in reply. 'We use our fingers like everybody else!'

Policewoman Titworthy had been abducted by assailants unknown and the chief inspector gathered his detectives around him to begin a full-scale hunt.

'The eyes of the world are upon us, and I want a speedy conclusion to the case,' he announced. 'I propose to bring in our crack police-dog Prince.'

Straining at the leash, the alsatian was brought before the assembled team, and a pair of Policewoman Titworthy's panties were produced from her locker.

'Right,' said the chief inspector. 'Let the dog sniff the panties!'

Prince nuzzled his nose into the missing policewoman's panties and started to yelp eagerly.

'OK – let him go!' yelled the chief inspector, and the dog shot out through the door. Ten minutes later it was back in the station – with the station sergeant's testicles in its mouth.

The telephone rang on the duty officer's desk at Bradford police station and the station sergeant answered it, to hear a frantic local landlord exclaim, 'Send a panda car round quick! There's a couple making love on the bar-room floor!'

'I bet the buggers are black,' said the officer.

'They are – but how did you know?' asked the landlord.

'Your bloody floors are *always* filthy,' replied the officer, and he hung up.

On a transatlantic flight on a Jumbo Jet, a British businessman was being pestered by the man sitting next to him who kept offering him cigarettes, whisky and a loan of his men's magazines.

'For the last time,' he burst out. 'I don't smoke, I don't drink and I don't read dirty books!'

A vicar who was sitting behind him leaned forward, tapped him on the shoulder and said, 'My dear fellow, I so admire your principles. Allow me to introduce my wife and daughter.'

'And I don't *screw* either!' he replied.

★   ★   ★

$$\frac{WREN}{SEXED} + AB = \frac{AB}{WREN}$$

$$\frac{WREN}{DUE} + \frac{AB}{SEAS} = \frac{WREN}{WROUGHT}$$

$$AB - £200 = WREN^2$$

★   ★   ★

A young man was explaining to a retired admiral that the old boy's daughter had been struggling in the sea, and he had pulled her on to his wind-surfing board and paddled back to the shore, where he had resuscitated her.

'Then, young man, you will have to marry her!' shouted the admiral.

★   ★   ★

A young man started work in a chemist's and his first customer asked for a bar of soap. The young man showed him the soap, wrapped it, and took the money. The chemist, who had been watching this brief transaction, was aghast.

'You can't serve customers as quickly as that!' he

exclaimed. 'Watch me and see how I do it.'

The next customer in the shop wanted a tube of toothpaste, and the chemist showed him a selection of brands and sizes, from which the customer selected one.

'Now sir,' said the chemist, 'would you like a new toothbrush too?'

'Yes, do you know I'd forgotten that!' said the customer, and went out of the shop quite happily with his purchases.

'There – do you see?' said the chemist. 'Always offer the customer something extra, and they might buy something more!'

The next customer in the shop, a man, asked the young assistant for a box of tampons. 'Certainly, sir,' said the assistant, 'and would you like a lawn mower too?'

Needless to say, the man left the shop somewhat hurriedly, and the chemist said to the assistant, 'What on earth did you ask him if he wanted a lawn mower for?'

'Well,' said the assistant. 'I figured as his weekend was f—ed up, he might as well cut the grass!'

★   ★   ★

During the Crimean War, a troop commander was visiting a front-line hospital to try to boost morale. At the first bed, he stopped and asked the soldier what his trouble was.

'Well, sir,' said the lad, 'the doctors say I've got syphilis.'

'Oh, dear,' said the commander. 'I'm sorry to hear that – what is the remedy?'

'I have to brush the affected parts, sir, and take some pills.'

'Well, man, let's hope you'll be up and about soon. And have you an ambition in life?'

'Yes, sir, to fight for my Queen and country!' came the reply.

The commander moved along the beds, and asked another soldier what *his* trouble was.

'Well, sir,' the soldier said, 'the doctors say I've got piles.'

'I'm sorry to hear that,' said the commander, 'what is the remedy?'

'I have to brush the affected parts, sir, and take some

pills.'

'Well, do whatever the doctors suggest, son. And have you an ambition in life?'

Yes, sir, to fight for my Queen and country!' said the soldier.

Further along the row of beds, the commander stopped again and asked a third soldier what his trouble was.

'Well, sir,' said the soldier in a whisper, 'the doctors say I've got laryngitis.'

'So I can hear,' said the commander. 'And what's the remedy?'

Painfully, the soldier croaked, 'I have to brush the affected parts, sir, and take some pills.'

'Good lad!' said the commander. 'And what's your ambition?'

'To get that f—in' brush before them others!' said the soldier.

★   ★   ★

Police in a panda car flagged down a motorist on a country lane.

'Sir, did you know your wife fell out of the car when you turned off the dual carriageway?'

'Oh, thank God!' said the man. 'I thought I'd gone deaf!'

★   ★   ★

A visitor to London asked a ticket collector at Waterloo for the time of the next train to Portsmouth.

'Seventeen forty-two,' said the ticket collector.

'Are you sure?' asked the visitor.

'Yes, madam. But if you don't believe me, ask my colleague at the next gate.'

So the lady went to the West Indian ticket collector and asked him the time of the next train to Portsmouth.

'Seventeen forty-two,' he said. 'And now you have it in black and white!'

★   ★   ★

What's the difference between EMI and the *Titanic?*
    The Titanic *had a better band.*

Do you know what really happened on board HMS *Victory* when Nelson was dying? He did, indeed, say 'Kiss me, Hardy!'

And Hardy replied, 'After all these years we've spent together on the same ship, *now* he asks me!'

— <u>NOW</u> HE ASKS ME!

What did the attendant in the chamber of horrors say?
'Keep moving along there please, madam. We're stock-taking!'

*   *   *

Once upon a time there was a little girl. She was just three years old, and had long blonde hair and sparkling blue eyes and a very pretty face.

One day she was taking her dog for a walk when she met the vicar.

'Hello, little girl,' said the vicar. 'What's your name?'

'My name's Petal,' replied the little girl.

'What a pretty name,' said the vicar. 'How did you come to be called Petal?'

'Well,' said the little girl. 'My mummy and daddy were longing to have a little baby, and then one day Mummy found that she was going to have one. It was summer time, and she was walking with Daddy in the garden, and a gentle breeze was blowing the petals off the roses. "I'm going to have a little baby," my mummy told my daddy. "That's wonderful news, darling," said Daddy. He looked round the garden at the drifting rose petals, and had an idea. "If it's a little girl we'll call her Petal." "Oh, yes," said Mummy "What a good idea." And that's how I came to be called Petal.'

'What a lovely story, said the vicar.' 'And what's your little dog called?'

'He's called Porky,' replied the little girl.

'And why's he called Porky?' asked the vicar.

'Because he f—s pigs.'

*   *   *

'Do you like bathing beauties?'

'I don't know, I've never bathed any.'

'Reuben, I understand you've had a big fire at your shop.'

'Sshh, Solomon, it's not until next week!'

'Who was that on the phone?'

'Wrong number. They must have wanted the Met Office –

they wanted to know if the coast was clear.'

'Have you ever slept with my wife?'
'Not a wink!'

'A kiss from you would be a real feather in my cap!'
  'Come outside, then, I'll make you Red Indian Chief!'

'How many people work in your office?'
'Oh, about half of us.'

'Nurse, have you told Mr Rogers his wife has had triplets?'
'Not yet, Doctor, he's still shaving.'

'My doctor's told me I have to give up half my sex life.'
'Which half are you giving up – talking about it or thinking
  about it?'

'I didn't come here to be insulted, you know.'
'Why – where do you usually go?'

'But why are you so angry?'
  'Oh, because it's all the rage.'

'Isn't that Hortense over there?'
'I thought she looked quite relaxed, actually.'

'Do you smoke after sex?'
'I don't know, I never looked.'

'We lay great stress on punctuation in this office.'
'Don't worry – I'm always at work on time.'

'Is the news bad, Doctor? How long have I got?'
'I'd suggest you don't start watching any soap operas.'

How can you tell the difference between a boy twin and a
  girl twin?
Look at the colour of their bootees.

✶ ✶ ✶

When Isaac lay dying his immediate family gathered round his bedside.

'Mama,' he whispered.

'I'm here, Isaac,' she replied.

'David,' he said.

'Here I am, Papa.'

'Ruth?'

'I'm here, Papa.'

'And Joseph?'

'I'm here too, Papa.'

'Then who in hell's name is minding the shop?'

* * *

Reuben walked into a supermarket and, passing the meat counter, asked the price of bacon. There was a huge flash of lightning followed immediately by an immense clap of thunder. Reuben went to the supermarket door, looked up and shouted, 'I was only asking!'

* * *

A little girl asked her mother whether she and her father had sexual relations. The mother, a little startled, replied, 'Why, yes, dear, we do. Why do you ask?'

'How come I haven't met any of them then?'

* * *

When their young son came home from school, his parents enquired how the first 'sex lesson' had gone.

'Oh, it was really boring,' said their six-year-old. 'We only did theory today.'

* * *

A businessman asked his secretary if she could ever forget the wonderful weekend they had just spent in Paris. 'What's it worth?' she asked.

* * *

Is it true that if you give up wine, women and song you live longer?

No, it just seems that way!

Happy is a moron –
He doesn't give a damn!
  I wish I were a moron –
Dear God! Perhaps I am.

Did you realize that Guy Fawkes was the only man ever to enter the Palace of Westminster with honourable intentions?

'If Mrs Thatcher were dead, I'd jump up and down on her grave!'
'I wouldn't – I hate queues.'

A man phoned a Third Division football ground and asked what time the match started.
  'What time can you get here?' he was asked.

A priest new to the parish told a young woman that he prayed for her each evening, to which she replied, 'There's no need for that – I'm on the phone!'

Have you heard the one about the farmer who put a silencer on his shotgun? His daughter wanted a quiet wedding!

If it's true that eight out of ten men write with a ball-point pen, what do the other two do with it?

My girlfriend has sex on the brain – I only love her for her mind.

The three ages of man are:
  TRI-WEEKLY; TRY WEEKLY; TRY WEAKLY.

Mounted police have it between their legs.

DIY experts do it with their hands.

Psychiatrists do it on the couch.

Cyclists do it in the saddle.

Lumberjacks do it with their choppers.

Netball players do it in three seconds.

Wind surfers do it standing up.

Dyslexics do it with a dictionary.

Teachers do it with class.

Telephone engineers do it in a hole.

Squash players do it against a wall.

Carpenters do it with their tools.

Doing It . . .

Lawyers do it in their briefs.

Professors do it by degrees.

The Mormon Tabernacle Choir do it all through the night.

Bartenders do it on the rocks.

Polo players do it on horseback.

Rugby players do it with odd-shaped balls.

Snooker players do it on cue.

Gardeners do it with green fingers.

Basketball players do it bouncing.

Organists do it pulling out all the stops.

Civil servants do it in triplicate.

Musicians do it with an instrument.

Town planners do it with their eyes shut.

'And how did you find yourself this morning?'
'I just rolled back the duvet, and there I was!'

What's the difference between a nice woman and the rubbish?

> *Rubbish gets taken out at least once a week.*

> *Roses are reddish,*
>   *Violets are bluish.*
>   *If it wasn't for Jesus*
>   *We'd all be Jewish.*

What happens if you eat too much fibre?

> *The bottom falls out of your world.*

Sex is like the monsoon – you never know how many inches you'll get or how long it'll last.

When is the safest time for sex?

> *When her husband's away.*

The only thing some married couples have in common is that they were married on the same day!

The family that prays together stays together – Thank God my mother-in-law is an atheist.

I knew a girl once who was so thin they rushed her to a maternity hospital when she swallowed a pea!

Do you know who make the best photographers?
People who snap at each other.

> *Amo, amas, I met a lass*
> *Who was very tall and slender*
> *Amas, amat, I laid her flat*
> *And played with her feminine gender.*

What do you get if you cross an onion with a donkey?
A piece of ass that makes your eyes water.

> *In Brighton, she was Bridget –*
> *She was Patsy up in Perth,*
> *In Cambridge she was Clarissa,*
> *The grandest girl on earth.*
> *In Stafford she was Stella –*
> *The best of all the bunch,*
> *But down on his expense account*
> *She was petrol, oil and lunch.*

'Mummy, what's an orgasm?'
'I don't know, dear – ask your father.'

What goes in dry, comes out wet, and gives enormous satisfaction?
A tea-bag.

Did you hear the one about . . .

the boss who fired his secretaries after a month because of mistakes they wouldn't make?

the farmer who went over his potato field with the heavy roller – he was trying to raise mashed potatoes?

the man who kept a portrait of his mother-in-law above the fireplace – to keep the children away from the fire?

the performer who'd been thrown off more stages than a Red Indian?

the latest pop group, who threw a stick of dynamite into the auditorium and brought the house down?

the Egyptian snake dancer, who couldn't tell her asp from her elbow?

Russian television – the *set* watches *you*!

the nudists who never go out on flag days?

the comedian who had to be *told* that laughter was a wonderful thing?

★ ★ ★

> *Two of Chalkie's relatives had a baby and they went to their church to have him christened. 'What do you want to call the baby?' asked the vicar. 'We want to call him Electricity,' said the mother. 'You can't call a baby Electricity. Why don't you call him Elijah or Moses?' 'Well, my name's Dinah and his name's Mo and dynamos make . . .'*

CHOW MEIN

or Nimble Nonsense

Chow Mein

Keeping an act fresh calls for a quick brain and a nimble tongue. I reckon in an hour to get through forty longish jokes, with lots of one-liners scattered in between, and having a good range of gags keeps the act fresh for me as well as the audience. It's important to be able to chop and change if things get a bit sticky and you get the impression that you're not going down too well. I remember one particularly hard week I had in Workington, playing a club where it was obvious the audience on the first couple of nights didn't like me very much. They laughed a little bit, but only enough to show that I was nearly dying on my feet. I wanted to get off, but I couldn't because the band weren't there to play me off and my dignity wouldn't let me just walk off the stage and admit defeat, so I plodded on, trying new lines and looking for jokes to get them on my side. By the Wednesday things were starting to look better and when I'd finished the management promised a good house for the following night. They were right too. After just ten minutes everything was going really well and I thought 'There's hope for me yet'. Then the door burst open and in came the local mayor and Prince Charles, who sat down to watch the act. So everyone turned their attention to him, and I had to work twice as hard to try and get them interested in me again. That's where having a good spread of gags always comes in handy.

Aristocratic Lady Jayne was holding a dinner party for her equally aristocratic (and snobby) friends when she suddenly and inadvertently broke wind very loudly.

'James,' she said, turning to her butler, 'stop that at once.'

'Certainly, ma'am,' replied the imperturbable butler. 'Which way did it go?'

★   ★   ★

Do you know why moths fly with their legs so far apart?
   No?
      Well, have you ever seen the size of a moth ball?

                        ★   ★   ★

A rabbi and a Roman Catholic priest were invited to attend
a civic function and were talking amicably when the
refreshments came round – a plate of sausage rolls. The
rabbi, obviously, declined, and the priest poked fun by
saying, 'Oh come now, rabbi. When are you going to relax
your religious beliefs enough to eat a little pork?'
   The rabbi smiled and replied quietly, 'At your wedding,
Father.'

                        ★   ★   ★

At an Arctic marine encampment the officers' mess was
being told about the elopement of one of the enlisted men.
   'But how could he elope, there isn't a woman for miles!'
said one of the officers.
   'He eloped with a polar bear,' replied the man's senior
officer.
   'Was it a female polar bear?' he was asked.
   'Of course it was! There's nothing odd about the men in
my company, you know!'

                        ★   ★   ★

I could never be a bigamist – imagine having two
mothers-in-law!

                        ★   ★   ★

> **Did you hear about the man who walked into the blood
> donor clinic and asked where he should spit his pint of
> blood?**

                        ★   ★   ★

My sister admits she has been happily married for five
years.

Not bad going, considering she's been married for twenty-five.

★ ★ ★

A man went to see his doctor, suffering from general ill health. The doctor examined him and asked him questions about his diet, and then about his life-style.

'Do you have many late nights?'

'No,' said the patient.

'Do you have sex?' asked the doctor.

'Infrequently,' said the patient.

'Is that one word or two?' asked the doctor.

★ ★ ★

A lady who had borne eight children went to her doctor to ask him for a hearing aid, saying she really did not want to have any more children.

'You need contraceptive advice, not a hearing aid,' said the doctor.

'No, doctor, I want a hearing aid. Every Friday night when my husband comes back drunk from the pub, he gets into bed and says, "Do you want to go to sleep or what?" I'm a bit deaf, and I always say, "What?"'

★ ★ ★

A man whose hand was smashed in a farming accident was fortunate to have a successful operation. The famous surgeon who grafted on the new hand explained, 'It may be a female hand, but it will work perfectly for you.'

A few months later, the patient returned, complaining to the surgeon that the hand was very good most of the time, 'But, being a female hand, whenever I go for a pee, it won't let go!'

★ ★ ★

A sailor went to see his doctor to complain about the doctor's diagnosis that his wife was pregnant.

'She can't be pregnant, doc – I've been at sea or away from home for the past year.'

Very gently, the doctor had to explain that this was what

was known as a 'grudge pregnancy'.

'What do you mean?' asked the sailor.

'Someone had it in for you,' replied the doctor.

* * *

A pretty young girl went to her doctor with a throat infection. As he was on holiday, she saw the replacement, who asked her to say, 'Ah!'

'That makes a change,' she said. 'Most men only ask me to say yes!'

* * *

Perturbed man in doctor's surgery: 'Doctor, you must help me! Every morning at seven o'clock I pass a motion – as regular as clockwork.'

Doctor: 'What's wrong with that?'

Patient: 'I don't get up until nine!'

* * *

A heart patient was summoned to see his consultant, who said, 'I've got some wonderful news for you! I've just received these special heart tablets from America – they're reckoned to be a miracle cure and will have you better in no time at all.'

'That *is* wonderful news,' said the delighted patient. 'When can I start taking them?'

'Take a blue tablet on Monday, and skip Tuesday. Take a green tablet on Wednesday, and skip Thursday. Take a red tablet on Friday, and skip Saturday and Sunday. Be very careful to follow these instructions exactly.'

A few weeks later the man's wife called on the consultant.

'Well, and how is the patient?' he asked her cheerily.

'Dead,' she replied.

'Dead?' said the consultant in disbelief. 'I can't understand it – those were the latest tablets. He should have been well on the way to full health. Didn't he follow the instructions?'

'It wasn't the tablets,' said the widow. '*They* were OK. It was all that bloody *skipping* that killed him.'

Suffering from a bad case of chapped lips, Paddy went to his doctor for a cure.

'What I want you to do,' said the doctor, 'is to get in your car, take a ride out into the contryside, and when you come to the first cow you see, lift up its tail and give its backside a good, long kiss.'

'Bejabers,' said Paddy. 'And will that be curing me chapped lips?'

'No,' answered the doctor. 'But it'll sure as hell stop you from licking them!'

★ ★ ★

'You've got to help me, doctor,' cried the anguished patient. 'I just can't stop passing wind. I have to do it every ten seconds and it's *so* embarrassing!'

'Take off your clothes and bend down, would you?' said the doctor. And he picked up a long wooden pole with a hook on the end of it.

'My God!' yelled the patient, wide-eyed. 'Whatever are you going to do with *that*?'

'I'm going to stand on your back and open the ruddy window!' replied the doctor.

★ ★ ★

A young man told his somewhat old-fashioned fiancée that he had dreamt of her the previous night.

'Did you?' she asked.

'No,' he replied, 'You wouldn't let me!'

★ ★ ★

Sign seen chalked on Forestry Commission land:

```
┌──────────────────────────────────┐
│                                  │
│        HAZEL WOOD                │
│     BUT JENNY WOULDN'T           │
│                                  │
└──────────────────────────────────┘
```

A very attractive young girl was stopped in the street by a young man who said, 'Haven't I met you somewhere before, beautiful?'

The girl glared at him and walked on.

'My mistake, lady!' said the man sarcastically, 'I thought you were my mother.'

'Impossible!' said the girl sharply. 'I'm married.'

What's love at second sight?
When the second time she meets you, a girl discovers you've got money.

How do you reply to a girl who says she never talks to perfect strangers?

'I never said I was perfect.'

A man was trying to seduce a beautiful blonde at a party and, thinking he was being successful, boldly asked her if she had ever been to bed with anyone before.

Haughtily, she replied, 'That's my business!'

Quick as a flash, the man said, 'Oh! I didn't realise you were a professional!'

Two friends were chatting on the telephone.

'I've got some wonderful news,' said Bob. 'She's finally said yes.'

'That *is* wonderful,' said his friend. 'When's the wedding day?'

'Wedding day? I didn't ask her to marry me!'

'Oh, Bob,' exclaimed the pretty girl. 'Mum wouldn't like it.'
'Your Mum's not getting it, is she!' replied her boyfriend.

There was a girl who wouldn't marry her boyfriend because of religious differences – he was poor, and she worshipped money.

★ ★ ★

I know a girl who was arrested on a Spanish beach for wearing a topless bikini. The policeman told her he was very sorry to take her in, because she did have two fantastic excuses!

★ ★ ★

A very well-built and attractive woman went into a church one day, only to be told by the vicar that he could not let her stay because she was improperly dressed.

'I have a divine right!' she protested.

'You have a beautiful left, too,' replied the vicar, 'but you still can't come in to my church.'

★ ★ ★

> **Did you hear about the girl with the hour-glass figure who slapped her boyfriend's face every time he put his arms around 9.15?**

★ ★ ★

What's the best two-piece outfit to give a gorgeous girl?
   A pair of stockings.

★ ★ ★

The day after his retirement party, Mr Johnson had to confess to his wife that they were going to have to live fairly quietly, 'We just won't have enough money for more than a few extras a year,' he explained. 'We won't be able to travel, or go to the cinema.'

'Don't you worry,' said his wife. 'I have a few thousand pounds saved up.'

'How have you saved so much?' asked Mr Johnson in amazement.

110

'Well, dear,' his wife explained hesitantly. 'Every time you made love to me, ever since we were married, I've put a pound in my bank account.'

'Well!' said Mr Johnson. 'If I'd known that's what you were doing, I'd have given you all my business!'

★　★　★

A bikini-clad girl was lying on her back soaking up the sun when a child walked by and accidentally dropped his ice-cream on to her stomach. Too lazy to sit up, she swore and said, 'Those damn seagulls must live in a freezer!'

★　★　★

A young member of the aristocracy married a true Sloane Ranger and on their honeymoon night he was naturally eager to take her to bed. He undressed very quickly and watched her undress. When she was completely naked, she opened her suitcase and took out a pair of long, black leather gloves, which she put on.

Thinking this was going to be a remarkable experience, he said, 'What are the gloves for?' and his bride replied, 'Mummy told me I might really have to *touch* your thing!'

★　★　★

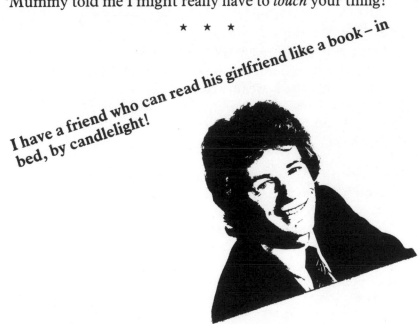

I have a friend who can read his girlfriend like a book – in bed, by candlelight!

111

A guest at a party was getting on rather well with a beautiful girl, and boldly asked the host if he might borrow his spare bedroom for a while.

'Yes, do,' replied the host, 'but what about your wife?'

'Oh, never mind the wife,' replied the guest. 'She'll never notice I've gone.'

'I know that,' said the host. 'She went into the spare bedroom ten minutes ago!'

★ ★ ★

At a fancy-dress party a young woman said to a man, 'I'm supposed to be a turkey. What are you supposed to be?'

'Chestnuts,' he replied.

★ ★ ★

On her way home after spending an evening with her boyfriend, a lady was stopped in her car by the police and asked to submit to a breath test. She blew into the breathalyser and instantly it changed colour.

'Well,' said the policeman, 'you certainly had a stiff one tonight.'

'Oh!' gasped the lady. 'Does it show that, too?'

★ ★ ★

A young man proposed marriage to a lovely young girl, and laid out all his credentials – he was good-looking, fit and the sole heir of his aged, wealthy father. The girl asked him for time to think over the proposal, and then wrote telling him that she couldn't marry him because she'd become his step-mother.

★ ★ ★

Two middle-aged men were discussing modern morals in the pub one evening.

'Never went to bed with my wife before we were married, you know. Wasn't the way to behave at all. Did you?' said one.

His companion replied, 'I don't know. What did you say her name was?'

★ ★ ★

An usher stopped a large, overdressed lady in the church porch before a wedding and asked if she was a friend of the bride's.

'No, I am not!' she hissed. 'I'm the mother of the groom!'

* * *

At a far outpost of the Foreign Legion a raw recruit was startled by the cry of, 'The camels are here! The camels are here!' Immediately, all the men rushed out of the fort to the approaching camel train.

'What's the hurry?' asked the recruit of one old hand.

'We use the camels for sexual purposes here. There aren't any women for a thousand miles,' the veteran said, starting to run.

'But what's the rush? There are enough to go around, surely!' said the young lad.

'Bloody hell, boy! You don't want an *ugly* one, do you?'

* * *

A young man watched as a girl walked towards him in a very tight pair of 'leggings' and high-heeled shoes. He couldn't help himself, and stopped her, saying, 'Excuse me. I don't mean to be rude, but I've never seen anyone in such tight clothes. How can anyone manage to get inside anything so tight?'

The girl smiled and said, 'Why don't you start by buying me a drink?'

* * *

A Scotsman in London for a day went to a prostitute in Soho. After he had been satisfied, he gave her one hundred pounds.

The prostitute was amazed, and said to the client. 'No one has ever given me a hundred pounds for my services before! And I thought you Scots were supposed to be tight with money. Whereabouts in Scotland are you from?'

'Aberdeen,' replied the man.

'Well!' said the prostitute, 'My father's from Aberdeen.'

'I know,' replied the man. 'When he heard I was coming

down to London, he asked me to give you a hundred pounds.'

★ ★ ★

A man asked his secretary to phone his wife and explain that he would be late home from the office because a visitor from overseas had arrived late and needed to be taken out to dinner.

When the secretary told him she'd delivered the message, the man asked, 'What did she say?'

The secretary replied, 'She said, "Can I rely on that information?"'

★ ★ ★

As the lift doors in a large hotel were closing on a crowded mass of people, the attendant asked, 'Which floors?'

A man called out, 'Ballroom, please!' and a lady instantly said, 'Oh, I'm so sorry. I didn't know I was squashing you that much!'

★ ★ ★

The definition of a sadist is someone who makes a hangman's noose out of barbed wire.

What is worn under a Scotsman's kilt?
Nothing is worn – it's all in A-1 condition!

★ ★ ★

—OF COURSE NOTHING IS WORN UNDER MY KILT, LASSIE—IT'S ALL IN A.1. CONDITION.

Chalkie bought a car – a brand new 1963 Vauxhall Cresta, a pink one with leopard-skin seats, spears on the roof-rack and a dog with a nodding head, all the trimmings. At the first set of traffic lights he stalled and broke down. But a nice policeman came along and said, 'I'll mend your car for you.' He lifted up the bonnet, had a tinker around and told Chalkie to start it up. It went first time. 'What was the matter with it?' asked Chalkie. 'Shit in the carburettor,' said the policeman.' 'How often have I got to do that?' Chalkie asked.

BANANA FRITTERS

or Feed Me a Line . . .

Banana Fritters

I like to try and shape my act in a way that keeps the audience happy by having a change of pace and delivery that flows through the whole hour or hour and a half, depending how long I'm on for. I try to hit them hard at the beginning, firing jokes at them until their ribs hurt, and then wind it down and chat to them once they've had a good laugh at the beginning. After that, I work into a long piece of really good jokes that they can remember, then perhaps a longish story, before hitting them really hard again at the end and finishing on a song. That way I manage to get off before the hook comes for me (most of the time anyway).

One of the best ways of making an audience's lungs hurt is a burst of good quick gags that have them splitting their sides on one joke while you're already telling the next. That way they never catch up and you leave them breathless and gasping for air – at least that's what you aim to do. So here to finish off are some of the quick-fire jokes I might use to give my act its final blast and I hope finish off my audience as well.

What four-letter word ends in 'k' and means intercourse?
Talk.

What do chiropodists like for breakfast?
Corn Flakes . . . and sometimes Shredded Feet.

What's the difference between Sex and Communism?
Communism is all left.

Who is the most popular girl in the school?
One who's been weighed in the balance and found wanton.

★   ★   ★

What's the definition of petting?
The study of anatomy in braille.

What's the definition of sex.
The most fun you can have without laughing.

What's better and even more restful than the sleep of the just?
The sleep of the just after!

How can you tell when you're in a honeymoon hotel?
All the couples are yawning by six in the evening.

What do you call a mobile Swedish massage parlour?
Feels on Wheels.

What's the difference between a pregnant woman and a light bulb?
You can unscrew a light bulb.

What is a Welsh rarebit?
A virgin in Rhyl.

Making love in a cornfield is going against the grain.

What happens to people who sleep like babies?
They never have any.

The biggest difference between men and women is their worry about the future – women worry until they get a husband, men never worry until they get a wife.

* * *

Beware the signs of old age: chasing girls, but forgetting why; and your mind making dates your body can't keep.

Who invented the jigsaw?
A Scotsman – when he dropped a fiver into a mincing machine.

What is the definition of an organ grinder?
A Durex full of sand.

What happened when the Irishman bought his wife a vibrator for Christmas?
She broke three of her teeth.

Why can't fairies get pregnant?
They only go to goblin parties.

* * *

How can you tell when you're colour blind?
When you put celery in the rhubarb pie.

Why did the Irishman run away from the hospital?
He saw a sign which said, 'Guide Dogs Operating Here'.

Why did 40 Pakistanis jump off a bus at Bradford when a white man got on?
They thought he was a ghost.

When are you and your wife most likely to be sexually compatible?
> *When you both have headaches.*

What happened when Cyril Smith fell into a crocodile pond at Regent's Park Zoo?
> *He ate three before they could drag him out.*

Why are Catholics with large families like British Rail trains?
> *They never pull out on time.*

Why don't gypsies use Durex?
> *Because they have crystal balls and can see it coming.*

* * *

What happened to the bridegroom who slipped on the bedroom floor?
> *He pole-vaulted out through the window.*

What's an undertaker's favourite TV programme?
> *Cask the Family.*

What are Junipers?
> *Hebrew children.*

How does a squirrel keep its nuts dry?
> *It swims on its back.*

* * *

Why doesn't Father Christmas have any children of his own?
> *Because he only comes once a year – and then it's down your chimney.*

* * *

> **Did you hear about the blind prostitute?**
> **You have to hand it to her ...**

What's purple and can get right to the scene of a murder?
A plum with a press pass.

Who has an IQ of 180 and green pubic hair?
Bamber Grassgroin.

Why do cannibals buy the ashes from crematoriums?
To use as Ready-Brek.

What did the hypochondriac have engraved on his
tombstone?
I told you I was bloody well ill!

★   ★   ★

What has the number 11 on its back, wears a uniform and
takes over the government of a country?
A right-wing military coup.

What did the Scottish landlord shout when he discovered a
bomb in his bar?
Last orders please.

What's black and white and goes round screaming?
A nun on a spit.

What is the definition of a Scottish gentleman?
One who gets out of the bath to pee in the sink.

★   ★   ★

Why aren't there any brothels in Ireland?
*Because the Irishmen used to stand outside all night
waiting for the red light to change to green.*

Who went to Mount Olive?
Popeye.

Why can't Frankenstein have any children?
Because his nuts are in his neck.

How do you circumcise a whale?

Send down foreskin divers.

What's the difference between snow-men and snow-women?
Snow-balls.

What did the hurricane say to the palm tree?
'Hold on to your nuts, baby – this is no ordinary blow job!'

What has a blue cap at one end and a pink cap at the other?
Hermaphraldite.

★   ★   ★

What's the definition of 'avoiding the issue'?
Contraception.

What did the actress say when the Bishop fondled her knee?
'Heaven's Above!'

What's the definition of a pansy?
Someone who likes his vice versa.

How do you make a hormone?
Don't pay her.

★   ★   ★

What is the definition of mistrust?
Two sailors in the showers with the soap on the floor.

What's a virgin sheep?
One that can run faster than a Welsh shepherd.

What's the definition of trust?
Two cannibals engaged in soixante-neuf.

What is the legal term for a man who mounts and stuffs animals?
A taxidermist.

What's another name for a wise-crack?
> *A virgin.*

What would you say to a girl who said she didn't know the difference between a chicken leg and a willy?
> *'Wanna come on a picnic?'*

Why were Adam and Eve believed to be Russian?
> *Because they had no clothes, only one apple for food, and they still thought they were in paradise.*

What's a Yankee Clipper?
> *An American Rabbi.*

* * *

What's the definition of a kept woman?
> *One who wears mink all day and fox all night.*

What's white and shuffles round the ballroom floor?
> *Come Dancing.*

Why was the Irishman carrying a sack of horse manure over his shoulder?
> *He won it in a crap game.*

What's white and goes up?
> *An Irish snowflake.*

* * *

What's an innuendo?
> *An Italian suppository.*

What's the world's shortest sex story?
> *Boy Scouts, Girl Guides.*

What do you call a Scouser in a Rolls Royce?
> *A thief.*

How can you tell you're at a Scottish wedding?
> *By the three-tiered scone.*

WHAT HAPPENS TO A FOOTBALLER
WHEN HIS EYESIGHT GOES?

HE BECOMES A REFEREE...

Why do they put a cock on a weather vane?
> *Because if they put a fanny up there, the wind would blow right through it.*

Why does the politician always wash twice in the morning?
> *Once for each face.*

What's the definition of a Russian Durex?
> *Little Red Riding Hood.*

★ ★ ★

How do you know when you're in a very small town?
> *The fire brigade is the local bed-wetter.*

What do you call a nun who limps?
> *Hopalong Chastity.*

What's the difference between a porcupine and a Volvo?
> *A porcupine has the pricks on the outside.*

What did the bus conductor say to the guy at the bus stop with no arms and legs?
> *Hello – how are you getting on?*

★ ★ ★

How do you make an Italian wine?
> *Kick him in the balls.*

What's the definition of a parasite?
> *Someone who goes through a revolving door without pushing.*

What's the difference between an egg, a carpet and sex?
> *You can beat an egg, you can beat a carpet . . .*

★ ★ ★

Why are sunburned girls like Christmas turkeys?
> *The white bits are the best.*

★ ★ ★

How can you tell an Italian aeroplane?
It's got hair under the wings.

How can you tell an Irish aeroplane?
It's got an outside lavatory.

What happened when Linda Lovelace met Charles
Aznavour?
She ended up with a frog in her throat.

What do you get if you cross an ant-eater with a vibrator?
An armadildo.

★ ★ ★

Why does an elephant have four feet?
He'd look daft with six inches.

What happens when you've got a really fat neighbour?
*When she hangs her washing out, you think the sun's in
eclipse.*

★ ★ ★

*Chalkie and his mate came out of a sex shop and
Chalkie said, 'I've just bought some of them contradic-
tives. You get three of them in a packet.' 'What did you
buy them for?' asked his friend. 'They're no good for a
black man. They're the wrong shape. They've got a little
bit on the end of them.' 'You silly git,' said Chalkie.
'That's what you put your foot on when you pull them
off.'*